THE PROPHECY OF DA

The Prophecy of Daniel

GOD RULES
IN THE KINGDOMS OF MEN

Edmund Green

THE CHRISTADELPHIAN
404 SHAFTMOOR LANE
BIRMINGHAM B28 8SZ

1988

First published 1988

ISBN 0 85189 122 5

PREFACE

THE Prophecy of Daniel is of the utmost fascination to students of the Bible. The stories of the man Daniel and his friends are of compelling interest to children from the earliest age; the prophecies offer a challenge to the most experienced. It is a book which a lifetime's study will never exhaust.

It is not surprising that one of the first 'works on the Truth' to be produced was John Thomas' *Brief Exposition of the Prophecy of Daniel*, first published in 1869—a work which has assisted several generations to a greater understanding of the prophecy. Brother Edmund Green's commentary stands alongside that former work (the author freely acknowledged his indebtedness to it) and offers fresh insight into the background and meaning of Daniel's visions. Its illustrations and time-charts will provide information at a glance on the major events of the period during which Daniel prophesied, and those that followed.

The purpose of prophecy is to warn the saints of "things which must shortly come to pass". The words may be "closed up and sealed till the time of the end" but sufficient has been made plain for us to be able to recognise the signs when they appear. Yet the words of the prophets are not merely there to provide us with signs; they are a source of encouragement, of comfort and exhortation. This commentary is published with the prayer that in both respects the household of faith may be helped in these last days.

In June, 1988, while the book was in the final stages of preparation, the author fell asleep in Christ in the confident hope that those who "sleep in the dust of the earth shall awake" (Daniel 12:2).

MICHAEL ASHTON

ACKNOWLEDGEMENTS

I AM grateful to my brother Ralph Green of Southampton, who read the first draft of my manuscript and made many constructive suggestions.

I also wish to acknowledge with thanks the help of David White, also of Southampton, in making improved versions of my Charts 1 and 2, illustrating the historical background of the period under review. Paul Wasson assisted with the maps, illustrations and cover design.

Bibliographic sources are acknowledged by footnotes and references in the text.

CONTENTS

PREFACE v

ACKNOWLEDGEMENTS vi

INTRODUCTION 1

CHAPTER 1: The Setting of the Prophecy 5

    APPENDIX I: The Historical Truth and Authorship of Daniel 10

    APPENDIX II: The Historical Background to Daniel 13

    APPENDIX III: Daniel 1:1 15

CHAPTER 2: Nebuchadnezzar's Image 17

    APPENDIX I: The Orders of Magicians etc. 24

    APPENDIX II: Critics' Views of the Four Empires 26

    APPENDIX III: "The God of Heaven" 27

CHAPTER 3: The Image of Gold 28

    APPENDIX I: The Detail in the Narrative 32

CHAPTER 4: The Dream of the Tree 35

    APPENDIX I: A Day for a Year 41

CHAPTER 5: Belshazzar's Feast 44

    APPENDIX I: Belshazzar and the Inscriptions 48

    APPENDIX II: Belshazzar: Some Circumstantial Detail 50

CHAPTER 6: The Lions' Den 52

    APPENDIX I: Darius the Mede 57

    APPENDIX II: The Lion Symbol 60

CHAPTER 7: The Four Beasts 61

    APPENDIX I: Papal Power 73

CONTENTS (continued)

CHAPTER 8: The Vision concerning the Daily Sacrifice 75

APPENDIX I: The Ram and the He-goat 83

APPENDIX II: The Son of Man 87

APPENDIX III: "Broken without hand" 89

CHAPTER 9: Daniel's Prayer—The Seventy Weeks 90

APPENDIX I: The Translation of Verse 24 101

APPENDIX II: The Word "Weeks" 103

CHAPTER 10: Daniel's Third Vision 104

CHAPTER 11: The Kings of the North and the South 112

APPENDIX I: "The Abomination that Maketh Desolate" ... 131

APPENDIX II: The Jews of Palestine, A.D. 70—1917 135

CHAPTER 12: Resurrection—"How Long?" 138

APPENDIX I: The Time Periods and the Decree of Phocas 148

APPENDIX II: The Time Periods: Moslem or Papal? 149

APPENDIX III: The Time Periods and Inspiration 154

EPILOGUE 156

NOTES ON THE CHARTS 158

CHARTS .... *To follow page 159*

ILLUSTRATIONS

General Map . . . .*Facing Page 1*

Nebuchadnezzar's Image and World Empires 19

The Beasts of Chapter 7 63

The Beasts of Chapter 8 77

CHARTS
To follow Page 159

CHART 1: Historical Background

CHART 2: Detailed History of Earlier Period

CHART 3: Restoration of Jerusalem unto Messiah

CHART 4: Daniel's Dream and Visions

CHART 5: Comparative Visions

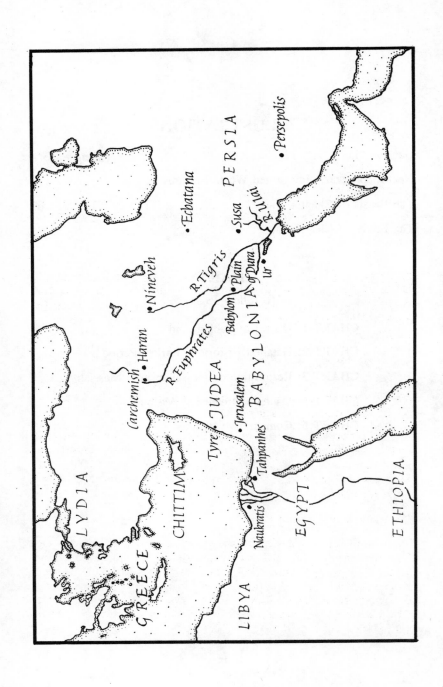

INTRODUCTION

DANIEL is an outstanding character. The divine testimony is that he is a man "greatly beloved" by God. Would that could be said of all of us! Daniel's account of his reaction to the various situations in which he found himself provides us with a glowing example of faithfulness.

Daniel the Man

This effort at the exposition of his prophecy is not a formal character study, but his experiences will impress upon our minds the attitude to life which is well pleasing to God.

Daniel's very long life of steadfastness, whilst enjoying material wealth, was fraught with tribulation and trial of faith. This is the atmosphere out of which God produced a prophecy which has stretched the minds of men who have loved God and His Word, both great and small, for hundreds of years.

The Historical Truth of Daniel

The book of Daniel contains prophecy and miracles on a grand scale. 'Unbelief' has therefore attacked its historicity. For those who believe that the Bible is the Word of God, there can be no doubt about the truth of the book, but it is well to take note of what the critics have said. We have summarised this in Chapter 1: Appendix I, but some of the objections that have been raised will be referred to in a general way as we proceed.

1

THE PROPHECY OF DANIEL

The Authorship and Unity of the Book

This aspect too is considered in Chapter 1: Appendix I. Suffice it to say here, that many of the sceptical ideas of early critics have had to be abandoned in the light of archaeological discoveries. Jesus himself confirmed the authorship of the prophecy in Matthew 24:15 and Mark 13:14. It is a curious fact that the author is unnamed in the first part of the book which is now generally admitted by scholars to date from the time about which it claims to have been written, whilst in the latter part, the authorship of which some still dispute, Daniel quite often writes in the first person: "I, Daniel . . . "

The Setting of the Book

The background details and atmosphere of the book also go a long way to establish its dating. Critics have to admit that the atmosphere and background are very definitely Babylonian and *not* Palestinian, which would have been the case, had it been written several centuries later in the Palestine of the Maccabaean epoch. There are no anachronisms. Lenormant (1837-83), a French archaeologist, is quoted as follows: "The colouring of the narrative is exactly Babylonian. The details of the manners and customs of the Babylonian court are given with an exactitude remarkably confirmed by the monuments, which no writer in Palestine of the 3rd or 2nd century B.C. could have possibly attained".[1] In discoveries of more recent times no facts have emerged which upset this verdict.

The Structure of the Book

There are two ways of viewing the subject matter of the book of Daniel and of dividing the book. Firstly, according to the language in which it is written; secondly, according to the substance—the dreams and activities of kings, and the visions of Daniel himself.

The language in which the book is written: From 1:1 to 2:4, and from 8:1 to the end, the book is written in Hebrew; the intervening portion from 2:5 to the end of chapter 7 is in Aramaic (called Syriac in the Authorised Version). Though it was a kindred tongue to Hebrew, Aramaic was the *lingua franca* among Semitic Gentiles of the times, spoken in Babylonia and in Israel also after the exile. It is therefore appropriate that the part of the book describing Gentile ascendancy

---

1. *Les Prem. Civil.*, i, p. 113; See *Speaker's Commentary*, "Introduction to the Book of Daniel", p. 231

and its final destruction, is expressed in the current Gentile language. This includes the beast dream of Daniel himself. That part which relates to the purpose of God with Israel, both in their subjection and in their final deliverance, is expressed in Hebrew.

The dreams and visions: The other way of dividing up the subject matter of the book arises from the fact that the first six chapters contain the dreams of, and narratives relating to, some of the kings of Babylon; whilst the remainder of the book consists of a dream and of visions seen by Daniel himself.

These two methods of division do not coincide. The first dream of Daniel about the four beasts is part of the Aramaic section but, having been revealed in the first year of Belshazzar, it overlaps historically the contents of chapters 5 and 6 which concern the overthrow of Babylon and the proclamation of Darius after the incident of the lion's den. Daniel's first personal revelation (chapter 7) is parallel with Nebuchadnezzar's first dream (chapter 2), in which the Gentile supremacy is depicted as being allowed by God progressively to over-run the earth, until the time appointed for the restoration of the Kingdom of God. The parallels between the two series of chapters are illustrated on Chart 5.

This interlocking scheme of two ways of dividing up the material, emphasises the unity of the book, the writing of which spans the whole period of Israel's exile in Babylon. In spite of all the evidence provided by study, scholarship and archaeology, demolishing subversive critical arguments, it is still a prevailing opinion in the popular mind that the book of Daniel is a product of the Maccabaean age, and that the prophecy was written after the event. Let our study of the book strengthen our faith, supported as it is by facts, which should dissipate the native scepticism of the natural man, based on prejudice.

The Historical Background to the Prophecy

In order to deal with this book in any comprehensive way, however briefly, it seems necessary to point out the major factors in the history leading up to, and lying behind, Daniel's ministry—especially as chapter 1 contains several difficulties when the text is studied closely. Fuller details of this historical background will be found in Chapter 1: Appendix II. Another interesting historical point is the identity of "Darius the Mede", concerning whom see Chapter 6: Appendix I.

3

THE PROPHECY OF DANIEL

So that readers may read the narrative continuously if they wish, background and other discursive material has been placed in appendices following each chapter. These can be read afterwards if preferred; and the whole work with Bible in hand please.

CHAPTER 1

THE book opens with a reference to the siege of Jerusalem by Nebuchadnezzar, in the third year of the reign of Jehoiakim:

"In the third year of the reign of Jehoiakim king of Judah came Nebuchadnezzar king of Babylon unto Jerusalem, and besieged it. And the Lord gave Jehoiakim king of Judah into his hand, with part of the vessels of the house of God: which he carried into the land of Shinar to the house of his god; and he brought the vessels into the treasure house of his god" (1:1-2).

It is a natural assumption that Daniel was taken captive when Jerusalem fell on this occasion. This raises a difficulty about the shortness of the time in which Daniel could achieve a three-year course of training and be in Nebuchadnezzar's service in time to interpret his dream by Nebuchadnezzar's second year (1:5; cf. 2:1). However, the text does not actually say *when* Daniel was made a captive; so it seems more likely that he may have been taken as a hostage at an earlier date (as suggested in Appendix III).

Verse 21 does not intend to tell us that Daniel continued no longer than the first year of Cyrus, but in effect says that he continued throughout the exile until the return of the Jews from the captivity under Sheshbazzar. He saw the whole 70 years of Babylonian supremacy foretold by Jeremiah. The N.I.V. rendering reads that "Daniel remained there until the first year of King Cyrus". If the inference is that then he left Babylon, it is noteworthy that the last vision that Daniel had in the third year of Cyrus was on the banks of the river Tigris over 50 miles away from Babylon.

Verses 3-20

The phraseology of the A.V. regarding the king's instruction to Ashpenaz, "And the king spake . . . ", does not necessarily involve that it was *consequent* upon what is referred to in verse 1, thus immediately involving Daniel and his three friends, but that it had *connection* with the same matter. In verse 3, Ashpenaz carries the title 'Master of the eunuchs' which is the same title given as Rab-saris in

5

2 Kings 18:17 and Jeremiah 39:3,13. Evidently he was a very important official who also accompanied the royal party on campaigns.

The rest of chapter 1 may be considered under three headings:

Verses 3-4: The Learning and Tongue of the Chaldeans;
Verses 5,8-16: Diet;
Verses 6-7,17-20: The Wisdom of Daniel and his Friends.

The Learning and Tongue of the Chaldeans: The institution of Palace Schools was a well recognised custom in Assyria and Babylonia. Tablets have even been found for the instruction of the young in their alphabet. In Assyria and Babylonia, though not in other countries, it also seems to have been a recognised practice to admit foreigners to these schools.

Since Nebuchadnezzar was a great warrior, it may be thought he was not likely to be interested in classical learning. This does not follow, and in fact such an idea would be far from the truth. It has been pointed out that "Babylonian learning and civilisation was far in advance of popular conceptions". In 1876 a collection of tablets called the Egibi tablets was found, which revealed the existence of a firm of bankers properly constituted with chairman, clerks, legal forms etc. Assurbanipal's library contained a huge encyclopaedia, embodying several kinds of dictionaries, treatises in law, chronological tables, a history of Nineveh and Babylon, a geographical encyclopaedia, civil service lists, revenue returns, works on natural history, arithmetic and astronomical observations, etc.[1]

Daniel could well accept training in such subjects without embarrassment. He may have been able to avoid 'magic', or at least have penetrated any deceptions involved in it, and not become involved.

The term "Chaldeans" is not the same thing as "Assyrians" or "Babylonians", although in some passages of Scripture it seems to be used interchangeably with them. In some connections it carries an *ethnic* meaning, and in some a cultural or *caste* significance. In the ethnic sense it represents a distinct ancient race, often called Akkadian, meaning mountaineers; the modern representatives of this race are called Kurds: they were once a most learned and civilised people. Urquhart says the use of their language had died out, and it was the object of the Palace Schools to revive this lost language.

1. J. Urquhart, *The Inspiration and Accuracy of the Holy Scripture*, pp. 359-375,494

In the 9th century B.C., a boasted pure Chaldee tribe began to become prominent in southern Babylonia, and became important enough to furnish kings of Babylon. These were called Kaldi, and as a class became the most powerful body in the kingdom, and were a superior and exclusive class like the priesthood were in Egypt; they used their office to control the State.

Tablets written in Akkadian were sometimes supplied with an Assyrian translation to make them intelligible to the common people. Thus it was easy in this sphere of learning to keep things secret and only allow them to be understood by the initiated, much as learned writers of a few hundred years ago wrote their important treatises in Latin. Such was the "learning and tongue of the Chaldeans" which Daniel and his three friends were taught.

The question is, Did Nebuchadnezzar himself belong to this ethnic group, seeing he was so interested in their tongue? It is now generally agreed that Nabopolassar and Nebuchadnezzar his son belonged to this ancient people. The "Chaldeans" were a caste as well as a nationality, and retained the tongue, writing and culture of their ancestors.

Diet: The record is not specific on this matter. Verse 5 refers to "the king's meat" and to his wine; verse 8 mentions the same items as a source of defilement to Daniel. There seem to be three possibilities:

(i) That the meat was cooked without draining out the blood, as required by the Law of Moses;

(ii) That it was 'unclean' meat—e.g. pork or horseflesh;

(iii) That it had been used in idolatrous religious rites and perhaps consecrated along with the wine to one of the gods.

Ezekiel 4:13 suggests that the Jews would find it impossible to keep the law in a Gentile environment, just as many Jews do today. In Daniel 11:26 the term "rich food" (R.S.V.) is the same as here, and partaking thereof carried covenant significance; so Daniel and his companions would, if faithful, feel obliged to avoid unqualified loyalty to Nebuchadnezzar. They ate pulse, a vegetarian diet, which stood them in good stead with Melzar their steward, for God blessed them with better health than those who partook of "the king's meat". Are there not lessons in this for us—right at the beginning of the book?

The Wisdom of Daniel and his Friends: In verses 6 and 7 we have new and foreign names given to Daniel and his compatriots. Although some think that there was no particular ideological principle involved

7

in this, merely the matter of convenience, it may be of interest to record
the meanings of the names as nearly as we can get to them. Having done
so, can we not detect a subtle attempt at antithesis?

Hebrew	Babylonian
God is my Judge—Daniel	Belteshazzar—Beltis* defend the king
God is gracious—Hananiah	Shadrach—I am very fearful (of God)
Who is as God?—Mishael	Meshach—I am of little account
God is a helper—Azariah	Abed-nego—The servant of (Nebo) the shining one

*Belet being a title for the wife of Marduk or
Bel, the patron of Babylon.[2]

Clearly God blessed these four young men with "knowledge and skill
in all learning and wisdom" and Daniel especially with understanding
in visions and dreams. This will emerge as we proceed in the chapters
which follow, although Daniel always humbly ascribed the interpretations to God. Nebuchadnezzar was duly impressed by the intelligence
of these four young Jewish men when he interviewed them.

Being brought up in the court of Pharaoh, "Moses was learned in all
the wisdom of the Egyptians, and was mighty in words and in deeds"
(Acts 7:22). But such a preparation did not draw him away from his
allegiance to the God of Israel, no doubt learned from his natural
mother in infancy. He was surprised that his enslaved brethren did not
understand that he was destined to deliver them from bondage, but in
his case a second term of 40 years was necessary to subdue his pride
and his reliance upon himself.

Nor were the four men before us drawn away by the classical learning of their day. Whoever was responsible, they too had been well
schooled in their very young days in the ways and Word of Yahweh
the God of Israel; consequently when faced with the learning of the
Gentiles, they did not depart from what they had been taught. Indeed,
it was their *anchor* which secured them safely, so that they could
remain steadfast, come what may. This is a point in favour of their age
of maturity before being taken captive. What Moses learned in isolation
in the desert, they learned in the testing heat of intrigue, and the temptations of court life. Their wisdom lay in *conviction*, that if they
remained faithful, God would be with them; whether He showed His

2. J. G. Baldwin, *Daniel*, Tyndale Commentaries, I.V.P.

8

hand openly or not, whether events appeared to move in their favour or not.

Here is the pattern for learning and for conduct in our day and age, both for parents and for children. How insistent our Heavenly Father is, in His revelation through Moses, upon the instruction of the young. His words were to be enshrined in their hearts, and they were to "teach them diligently unto thy children, and shalt talk of them when thou sittest in thine house, and when thou walkest by the way, and when thou liest down, and when thou risest up . . ." (Deuteronomy 6:7). One could wish that such conversation was more prevalent now.

CHAPTER 1: APPENDIX I

The Historical Truth and Authorship of Daniel

Sad to say, it is largely professedly Christian clergy who have contended against the historicity of the book of Daniel. Fortunately the book has not been without its defenders who have drawn attention to its divine character, the illogical arguments used against it, and the evidence of archaeology in its favour. One of these, E. B. Pusey, pointed out unsparingly that it was the disbelief in the possibility of foretelling the future, and of miracle, that was the inspiring motive in those criticising the book, and not that its faults were such as to leave them no alternative, as some claimed.

Dr. Pusey, writing in 1864, comments: "True, disbelief of Daniel had become an axiom in the unbelieving critical school. Only, they mistook the result of unbelief for the victory of criticism. They overlooked the historical fact that the disbelief had been antecedent to the criticism. Disbelief had been the parent, not the offspring of their criticism; their starting-point, not the winning-post of their course".[1]

Dr. Pusey commences the first of his Nine Lectures in reply to the then current criticisms, with these trenchant words: "The book of Daniel is especially fitted to be a battlefield between faith and unbelief. It admits of no half-measures. It is either Divine or an imposture. To write any book under the name of another, and to give it out to be his, is, in any case, a forgery, dishonest in itself, and destructive of all trustworthiness. But the case as to the book of Daniel, if it were not his, would go far beyond even this. The writer, were he not Daniel, must have lied, on a most frightful scale, ascribing to God prophecies which were never uttered, and miracles which are assumed never to have been wrought. In a word, the whole book would be one lie in the Name of God. The more God, as we shall see, is the centre of the whole, the more directly would the falsehood come into relation to God."

The critical contention was concentrated in making out the authorship to be as late as possible, that is post-exilic; that the book was a product

---

1. E. B. Pusey, *Daniel the Prophet: Nine Lectures*, Preface, p. vi

of the Maccabaean era, written by a pious Jew for the encouragement of his associates suffering from the effects of the wars between the Egyptian Ptolemies and the Syrian Seleucids, and persecution at the hands of the henchmen of Antiochus Epiphanes. This had been the argument of Porphyry (ca. A.D. 232-305), whose destructive efforts would have been forgotten but for the quotations noted by Jerome (ca. A.D. 345-419) in his answers to the controversy at that time. Porphyry's disbelief in prophecy and miracle was revived in the early 18th century by many 'Christian' clerical scholars.[2] The dates during which Daniel could ostensibly have been written, would have been between the captivity of Daniel early in the reign of Nebuchadnezzar (ca. 607 B.C.), and just subsequently to the date of the last vision, which is given as the 3rd year of Cyrus (ca. 536 B.C.): in other words, the time span of the exile. The date of its supposed production in the Maccabaean epoch is 168-7 B.C. (S. R. Driver), nearly four centuries later. Some writers claim Daniel was written not earlier than 300 B.C.[2]

John Urquhart (1895), another writer in defence of the book of Daniel, exposed the error of the arguments of Dean Farrar (Archdeacon, Canterbury ca.1895), among others, who claimed: "There was no king Belshazzar; there was no Darius the Mede who preceded Cyrus as king and conqueror of Babylon".[3] He also attributed to Daniel other things that his book does not say.

It is obvious that Daniel does not purport to give a history of Babylon, but only refers to rulers who were key figures in the revelation and development of God's purpose with mankind.

The Authorship and Unity of the Book

As a result of the controversy and of archaeological discoveries, it has largely been conceded that chapters 1-6, and perhaps 7, are of early date; but chapters 8-12 are still by some considered to be of late date. Yet there is no evidence in the book of more than one author, nor of differing viewpoints. The chief objection revolves round chapter 11 as to whether it is prophecy, or was written after the event. If the latter were true, one would think that the author would have mentioned the characters involved by name. The pros and cons are summed up from the point of view of writers on the subject in the *Tyndale Commentary*, where a strong case is made out for a single author.[4]

2. J. G. Baldwin, *Daniel*, Tyndale Commentaries, I.V.P., pp. 64, 18
3. J. Urquhart, *The Inspiration and Accuracy of the Holy Scripture*, p. 553
4. J. G. Baldwin, *Daniel*, Tyndale Commentaries, I.V.P., pp. 38-43

The fact also has to be taken into account, that the Septuagint version, the Greek translation of the Old Testament Scriptures, was already in existence in Maccabaean times.[5] Tradition has it that this version was made in Alexandria by about 70 Jews on behalf of Ptolemy Philadelphus (ca. 280 B.C.), and completed not long after. (It is known as the LXX.) It contained the book of Daniel, but as Pusey points out, this version contains many modifications and differences from the Hebrew original, apparently made out of deference to the susceptibilities of current Egyptian public life—the omission in Daniel 5:3-4 of reference to wives and concubines being a case in point.[6]

This fact in itself calls for a still earlier date for the Hebrew original. This version was so mutilated, that Jerome tells us that the Church rejected it, and a later version by Theodotian was used in its place.[6] Even if Daniel 8-12 was produced shortly before the Maccabaean wars of ca. 165 B.C., it is extremely difficult, if not impossible, to conceive that such a spurious work could have been generally accepted as canonical so as to have been incorporated into the LXX version so quickly, when everyone would know that it was a recent production.[7]

Several small sections of Daniel (derived from the Hebrew, not from the LXX version) occur in fragments of the Dead Sea Scrolls, which scholars date as written up to 100 B.C. From these and other Qumran scrolls it is deduced that Daniel was regarded in the Qumran sect as of great authority; and that a considerably greater antiquity for the original than Maccabaean times is presupposed.[8]

A study of the Aramaic language of Daniel also suggests an early date. Kitchen reaches the conclusion that "the Aramaic of Daniel (and Ezra) belongs to the early tradition of Imperial Aramaic (seventh-sixth to fourth centuries B.C.) as opposed to later and local Palestinian derivatives of Imperial Aramaic".[9] *The Speaker's Commentary* also says, "Criticism of the Hebrew and Aramaic section is, philologically considered, opposed to the Maccabaean date".

5. J. Urquhart, *Wonders of Prophecy*, p. 136
6. E. B. Pusey, *Daniel the Prophet: Nine Lectures*, p. 624
7. J. G. Baldwin, *Daniel*, Tyndale Commentaries, I.V.P., pp. 44-46, 63-71
8. J. G. Baldwin, *Daniel*, Tyndale Commentaries, I.V.P., p. 73
9. K. A. Kitchen, *Notes on Some Problems in the Book of Daniel*, pp. 31-79

CHAPTER 1: APPENDIX II

The Historical Background to Daniel

At the relevant epoch in history there were two super-powers, Egypt and Babylonia; the latter had only recently superseded Assyria in this capacity. Pharaoh-Necho emerged from Egypt in 609 B.C. to attack Babylonian forces on the Euphrates in support of Assyria, but the Judaean king Josiah intervened and was killed in battle by the Egyptians (2 Kings 23:29—24:7). The people of Israel put his son Jehoahaz on the throne, but he only lasted three months. In the meantime Necho, proceeding north, had joined an Assyrian king Assur-uballet, crossed the Euphrates and engaged a Babylonian garrison stationed in Haran. On his return three months later, Necho took Jehoahaz prisoner to Egypt and replaced him with his brother Eliakim, changing his name to Jehoiakim. All this was in 609 B.C.

Early in 606 B.C. Egypt was still having success in the Euphrates area, and Nabopolassar the Babylonian king counter-attacked; but in the next year (605) he died. His son Nebuchadnezzar had already taken over the leadership of the armed forces, and was busy campaigning against Necho. He inflicted a disastrous defeat on him at Carchemish which delivered into his hands "the whole area of the Hatti country". That is what the Babylonian Chronicle calls the area of Syria southwards to the borders of Egypt. It was whilst engaged in this conquest that Nebuchadnezzar heard of his father's death. Sending his prisoners and heavy equipment to Babylon by the normal route, Nebuchadnezzar himself pushed across the desert and occupied the throne of Babylon 21 days after the death of his father.

This year 605 B.C. is the year mentioned in Daniel 1:1 as the third of Jehoiakim and in Jeremiah 25 as the fourth. There is no real discrepancy, as will be seen later (Appendix III). Jehoiakim became Nebuchadnezzar's servant for three years, and then rebelled. This servitude may have been the result of the "siege" mentioned in Daniel 1:1. In 601 Nebuchadnezzar fought a great battle in Egypt where he suffered defeat, and he remained at home in 600. Through 599, 598 and 597 he was occupied a second time in subduing Syria and Palestine and besieging Jerusalem.[1] He made Jehoiakim prisoner with the object of taking him to Babylon. It is not clear when this was, but by some means not described, Jehoiakim died, apparently before he could be transported to Babylon; and his body was cast out of the city, "buried with the burial of an ass" at Jerusalem, as Jeremiah had prophesied (2 Chronicles 36:6; Jeremiah 22:18-19).

This brings us to the short reign of Jehoiachin (three months), to his captivity, and to the installation of Zedekiah on the throne of Judah. We know that Zedekiah was taken prisoner to Babylon 11 years later, when, after a siege of three years, Nebuchadnezzar destroyed Jerusalem. The Judaean kingdom did not exist for 70 years, and another captivity ensued. Jeremiah in Jerusalem and Ezekiel in Babylonia both deal with these events, but Daniel in the city of Babylon is strangely silent about them.

Nebuchadnezzar reigned about 43-44 years. He was succeeded by his son Evil-Merodach (or Amel-Marduk) and several other kings not mentioned in the book of Daniel. Evil-Merodach was the king who was kind to Jehoiachin and eased his imprisonment (2 Kings 25:27; Jeremiah 52:31). This first year of Evil-Merodach is equated with the 37th year of the captivity. He was assassinated after two years on the throne. Next came Neriglissar, former Rab-Mag (Chief of the Magi), who married a daughter of Nebuchadnezzar, and reigned for three years. His young son Labaroso-archod (or Labashi-Marduk) was assassinated by the nobles after only a few months' reign. In his place the nobles elevated Nabonidus who reigned for 17 years, but since he was away from Babylon for much of this time, his son Belshazzar was the acting king.

A veil is drawn over Daniel's activities during these events. Belshazzar was slain when the forces of Cyrus took the city, but Nabonidus, not being present, survived the fall of the city for some years. There is a slight variation in the dating of these kings' reigns between the British Museum List, the *Tyndale Commentary* [2] and other authorities.

---

1. E. R. Thiele, *Mysterious Numbers of the Hebrew Kings*, pp. 165-167
   J. G. Baldwin, *Daniel*, Tyndale Commentaries, I.V.P., pp. 19,20
2. J. G. Baldwin, *Daniel*, Tyndale Commentaries, I.V.P., p. 73

CHAPTER 1: APPENDIX III

Daniel 1:1

There are some difficulties associated with the records in verse 1.

(a) There is no reference in the historical books of Scripture to an attack on Jerusalem by Nebuchadnezzar in the third year of Jehoiakim. We are simply told that he became servant to Nebuchadnezzar three years and then he rebelled (2 Kings 24:1-2). But since Nebuchadnezzar was in conflict with Egypt, it must be assumed that he would take in his stride all who were under the influence of Egypt, as was Jehoiakim. The reference to the fourth year of Jehoiakim is in Jeremiah 25:1; 46:2, and applies to the battle of Carchemish. This apparent disparity is due to a difference between Egyptian and Babylonian modes of computation.

"The one most usual in the history books of the Old Testament counts the months between the king's accession and the new year as a complete year, whereas the method most usual in Babylon called those months the accession year, and began to count the years of the king's reign from the first new year. The date in Daniel would appear to have come from a source compiled in Babylon and those in Jeremiah from a Palestinian source, but rightly understood there is no discrepancy".[1]

(b) The third year of Jehoiakim was before Nebuchadnezzar became king of Babylon, so we have to postulate either that Nebuchadnezzar had been made co-regent with his father, or that the record being written at a later date, he was called "king" because he was king at the time of writing.

(c) Since the captivity of Daniel appears to have resulted from a "siege" of Jerusalem in 605 B.C., and since Nebuchadnezzar's dream was given in the second year of his reign, there is insufficient time for the three years training in Chaldaic lore, as required by Daniel 1:5, before Daniel was called to appear before Nebuchadnezzar to interpret the dream. One resolution of this difficulty is to invoke the idea that

---

1. J. G. Baldwin, *Daniel*, Tyndale Commentaries, I.V.P., p. 21

two partial years are counted as whole ones,[2] which is not very convincing in the circumstances.

There is another possibility. As we noted when dealing with verses 1, 2 and 21, although it is a natural inference, the text does not specifically state that Daniel was made captive in the third year of Jehoiakim. Could he have been taken to Babylon as a hostage at an earlier date? Verses 17-20 seem to imply that Daniel and his friends completed their full term of training before being placed in the king's service. Their danger at the time of the failure of the Chaldeans to interpret Nebuchadnezzar's dream also implies that they were in full service.

The references to Jehoiakim in the historical books are rather vague as to time. In 2 Kings 24:1-2 it is related that "in his days" Nebuchadnezzar "came up" and Jehoiakim became his servant three years and then rebelled; also "the Lord sent bands of the Chaldees" and others against him. Verse 7 says that Nebuchadnezzar had taken all the territory that "pertained to the king of Egypt" which would include Judaea. None of these events is precisely dated; some of them could have been before Jehoiakim's third or fourth year. 2 Chronicles 36:6 says that Nebuchadnezzar came up and "bound Jehoiakim in fetters, to carry him to Babylon". It does not say in which year of his reign, nor is there any record that he ever went to Babylon; but it seems almost certain that there was a second siege to quell his rebellion. It would also seem that this rebellion would coincide with the reverse Nebuchadnezzar suffered in Egypt in 601 B.C.

Since Jehoiakim was Pharaoh-Necho's protégé, and Nebuchadnezzar was campaigning against Necho in the Euphrates area for several years before the decisive battle of Carchemish, it seems possible that he would try to bottle up Jehoiakim and immobilise him by some sort of "siege" of Jerusalem, in order to protect his flank before 605 B.C. Scripture does not state this, but neither does it appear to exclude the possibility. It is quite possible, therefore, that hostages may have been taken from Jerusalem at an earlier date than 605, to try and secure the good behaviour of Jehoiakim towards Nebuchadnezzar. If this be admissible, it would allow more time for the instruction of Daniel and his friends, had they been among hostages taken in this way. Furthermore, in view of Jehoiakim's antipathy towards Jeremiah and the Word of the Lord, he may have been quite happy to part with a group of young men devoted to the God of Jeremiah.

2. J. G. Baldwin, *Daniel*, Tyndale Commentaries, I.V.P., p. 85

CHAPTER 2

THIS second chapter reveals the famous dream which so disturbed the sleep of king Nebuchadnezzar. His reaction in calling in his wise men to explain it enables us to look very briefly at the categories into which they were divided (Appendix I). The first two classes had already been referred to in 1:20, and, as translated in the A.V., are "magicians and astrologers". Chapter 2:2 adds "sorcerers and Chaldeans": verse 27 further adds "wise men and soothsayers".

Such were the characters assembled before Nebuchadnezzar, whom he obviously mistrusted and suspected of conspiring to tell him "lying and corrupt words" (verse 9). Nebuchadnezzar was determined to put these learned men to the test. If he could make them tell him the dream, he would know that they would have the insight to interpret it.

Nebuchadnezzar's phrase, "the thing is gone from me", is interpreted by some to mean that he had forgotten the dream. Others understand it to mean that it was the decree of severe penalty for failure to describe and interpret the dream that had gone forth from the king, and which he refused to withdraw, despite the apparent unreasonableness of his request. No doubt the king reasoned that if their learned claims were genuine, they would be able to 'divine' what the dream was; their failure would prove they were charlatans. The N.I.V. renders verses 7-9 thus:

"Once more they replied, 'Let the king tell his servants the dream, and we will interpret it.' Then the king answered, 'I am certain that you are trying to gain time, because you realise that this is what I have firmly decided: if you do not tell me the dream, there is just one penalty for you. You have conspired to tell me misleading and wicked things, hoping the situation will change. So then, tell me the dream, and I will know that you can interpret it for me'."

The disclaimer of the astrologers and the rest is, "What the king asks is too difficult. No-one can reveal it to the king except the gods, and they do not live among men" (N.I.V.). This brought the full wrath of the king down upon them, and the promulgation of the decree to be enforced against them by Arioch—which involved Daniel and his friends, since they were also members of this hierarchy. The situation thus created sends Daniel to his God in prayer jointly with his three friends; and so the Divine purpose in causing the dream is achieved through the revelation of its details to Daniel who had secured a 'stay of execution', to permit of this prayerful purpose.

Not only are this prayer and the revelation it brings impressive, but so is Daniel's reverent ascription of praise to God, who "reveals deep and hidden things" and had given Daniel "wisdom and power". So Daniel returns to Nebuchadnezzar to give him the revelation of his dream and the interpretation as well, and the lives of all the "wise men" are saved.

Nebuchadnezzar's Dream

After remarking that the wise men in their several categories were unable to reveal the secret, yet the God in Heaven had done so (see Appendix III), Daniel continued:

"As for thee, O king, thy thoughts came into thy mind upon thy bed, what should come to pass hereafter: and he that revealeth secrets maketh known to thee what shall come to pass. But as for me, this secret is not revealed to me for any wisdom that I have more than any living, but for their sakes that shall make known the interpretation to the king, and that thou mightest know the thoughts of thy heart" (2:29-30).

Thus the object of the revelation is twofold. It is for the sake of those who reveal the interpretation, Daniel and his friends, as well as for the information of Nebuchadnezzar. Would not the first object include future friends as well? Modern versions omit the phrase "for their sakes", but it seems an appropriate thought. The "things written aforetime" were "for our admonition", "for our learning, that we through patience and comfort of the Scriptures might have hope" (1 Corinthians 10:11; Romans 15:4).

What Daniel tells Nebuchadnezzar he saw in his dream is called in the A.V. an "image"; the N.I.V. renders the word as a "statue". It is not meant to represent an idol for worship. As the picture unfolds, it becomes evident that whatever the meaning might be, what he saw was the form of a *man*. This is not only appropriate to the question in Nebuchadnezzar's mind, but it also is significant. Most Biblical representations of nations take the form of animals; they do so in Daniel's own book, in chapter 7 for example. The representation in Daniel 2 of a *man* is unique.

BABYLONIAN EMPIRE

Head of Gold

PERSIAN

Breast and Arms of Silver

GREEK

Belly and Thighs of Brass

ROMAN

Legs of Iron

Feet of Iron and Clay

19

God's purpose primarily concerns *men*. Daniel's name means 'God is Judge'—He is judge of men. Later we shall find emphasis laid upon the principle that "God rules in the kingdom of *men*". When Nebuchadnezzar erected a literal colossal image of gold, as related in chapter 3, that too is usually understood to be the image of a man—probably of Nebuchadnezzar himself. In chapter 10 Daniel has a vision of "a certain man" (margin, one man), clothed in linen. It is not yet time to enter upon exposition of this chapter, but it is becoming clear that this book is specially relevant to God's relations with man, *Gentile as well as Jew*.

In Nebuchadnezzar's dream, a composite *man* represents successive world powers collectively considered. This man also represents singularly one mortal but pride-inflated ruler. By contrast, in Daniel's vision, "One Man" represents collectively a spiritual multitude redeemed and saved by the single *Man*, Messiah the Prince, who appropriates the title "Son of Man".

We are not left to inference or human theory to explain the dream revealed by Daniel in 2:31-35. God Himself supplies the interpretation and it is related by Daniel to Nebuchadnezzar in verses 36-45. Inasmuch as God, "the God of heaven", had made Nebuchadnezzar world-wide ruler, *he* was the golden head of this awe-inspiring colossal statue. The chest and arms of silver are dismissed with the words "after you, another kingdom will rise, inferior to yours". The belly and thighs were made of bronze, a less valuable metal still which represented a third kingdom that would rule over the whole earth. "Finally there will be a fourth kingdom, strong as iron" represented by the two legs—iron, which breaks and smashes all kingdoms into submission. The weakness of human authority and rule is represented in the last stage; the feet and toes—"partly of iron and partly of baked clay; so this kingdom will be partly strong and partly brittle . . . the people will be a mixture and will not remain united, any more than iron mixes with clay" (verses 42,43, N.I.V.).

The first observation to make upon this description is that there is a succession of four Imperial periods—the first representing Nebuchadnezzar himself, who in turn stands for his Babylonian Empire and his dynastic successors. The second observation is that the metals represent kingdoms destined to rule over the whole earth. Thirdly, the last (iron) stage, starting in full strength, would end up weak by reason of division and lack of cohesion between otherwise strong components. The prophecy of Daniel itself was written contemporarily with only the first two stages, although the third is named in later prophecies. So we have to turn to secular history to supply the subsequent fulfilment of what the prophecy reveals cryptically concerning them.

The first two stages were obviously the Babylonian and Persian supremacies; the third (referred to in Daniel 8:21 by name), was clearly the soon to be rising Greek power. It does not seem possible to doubt that the fourth was the Roman power; especially in view of its historical development in two sections, corresponding with the legs, and to the divided state which has obtained for so long since. The Stone by which it is to be destroyed has not yet fallen upon it. (The critics' view of this interpretation is outlined in Appendix II.)

We conclude, then, that the image in this dream represents a slowly developing symbolic man, with a golden federal head. Although it is said of Nebuchadnezzar, "Thou art this head of gold", the golden head cannot be *confined* to him personally. The silver section of the image was not joined on until years after his death, and other Babylonian kings ruled after him. The Golden Babylonian empire survived him for some 25 years.

The head inspires the whole human body; thus although racial leadership changes through four Imperial stages, in the prophecy the whole is viewed as a unit, and in the end is destroyed together by the stone. Therefore the golden head, Nebuchadnezzar, typical of the whole, persists in some sense as the motivation of the kingdoms of men. The head, being the ruling or animating principle, stands for human despotism and apostasy from the True God. Each power represented by a metal had existed independently for a long time before being associated with the image. The time of their acquisition of the city of Babylon is the point of their conjunction with the image. Continuity consists in lordship of that territory, until its ruin (as prophesied) in Seleucid times.

Although these empires are said to "bear rule over all the earth", they were not *literally* worldwide, but comprised what was thought of as the civilised world of their time. More particularly, each held sway over the land of Israel which was affected by the successive dominations.

The Kingdom of God
The kingdom of God is to succeed human decay, inefficiency and wickedness. It is not to consist of a Church ruling over men's hearts

in the midst of the world's political organisations. Daniel's words could hardly be plainer or more literal.

"In the days of these kings shall the God of heaven set up a kingdom, which shall never be destroyed: and the kingdom shall not be left to other people, but it shall break in pieces and consume all these kingdoms, and it shall stand for ever. Forasmuch as thou sawest that the stone was cut out of the mountain without hands, and that it brake in pieces the iron, the brass, the clay, the silver, and the gold; the great God hath made known to the king what shall come to pass hereafter; and the dream is certain, and the interpretation thereof sure" (2:44-45).

The stone "cut out of the mountain without hands", that is without *human* hands, is by inference a power provided by Divine means. "Not by might, nor by power, but by my spirit, saith the Lord of hosts" (Zechariah 4:6), expresses a principle recurring in Daniel and other prophecies, as we shall see. The stone itself is also a recurring figure which is applied to Jesus in the New Testament (e.g. Isaiah 8:14; 28:16; Romans 9:33; 1 Peter 2:4-8 etc.). Jesus is the "Great King" in the new system to be set up when "the God of heaven shall set up a kingdom which shall never be destroyed", but which will break in pieces all the human political organisations currently existing; and when Jerusalem becomes the centre of his rule (Matthew 5:35).

Nebuchadnezzar was duly impressed by what he heard, and no doubt flattered by the allusion to himself as being the golden head, so he renders homage to Daniel and to his God, as verse 46 records;

"Then the king Nebuchadnezzar fell upon his face, and worshipped Daniel, and commanded that they should offer an oblation and sweet odours unto him. The king answered unto Daniel, and said, Of a truth it is, that your God is a God of gods, and a Lord of kings, and a revealer of secrets, seeing thou couldest reveal this secret."

Daniel thereupon receives valuable gifts and promotion to a position of power over the entire province of Babylon. He also takes advantage of the king's good mood to speak up for the three friends who had cooperated in his prayers, and they too are given high office.

We are not told of the reaction of the other "wise men", but human nature being what it is, we can imagine that the relief gained by the sparing of their lives was deeply tinged with jealousy of Daniel. If so, it was a very long time before they were able to turn the tables on him—but perhaps it was the next generation who lost their lives in the attempt.

CHAPTER 2: APPENDIX I

The Orders of Magicians etc.

The excavations of the archaeologists have unearthed many inscriptions that have added a great deal to human knowledge concerning Babylonian and other ancient nations. For present purposes the briefest description will be adequate; fuller information can be found in various books of reference if needed.

Magicians: The word in the original is also applied to the soothsayer priests of Egypt, and indeed may come from an Egyptian root (cf. Genesis 41:8; Exodus 7:11). Their chief function seems to have been to exorcise demons and evil spirits by incantations, prayers and imprecations. The magicians are credited with a sacred literature consisting of magical texts or incantations (some of which were recited in a whisper), hymns and penitential psalms. This group included conjurors. Isaiah 8:19 refers to wizards "that peep and that mutter"; the word for "peep" is elsewhere translated "chatter" and "whisper". The whole activity is roundly condemned by God in Leviticus 19:31; 20:6,27 etc.

Astrologers: The original word here is sometimes rendered "enchanters". They are called "theosophists" and were noted for communicating by means of hymns, with mystic and supernatural powers, and the use of a muttering manner of speech. Their function seems to have consisted in counselling and foretelling the destinies of men.

Sorcerers: The original word is from the same root as for magicians, and also refers to witchcraft; and similarly, they were mutterers of magic formulae.

Chaldeans: As we have already seen, these Kaldi or Casdim derived their name from an ancient tribe in southern Babylonia; but the name later acquired a caste significance by reason of the academic type of people they were; thus they gave their name to a sort of priesthood. Their literature included all sorts of omens, magic incantations, prayers, hymns, myths and legends; scientific formulae for skills such as glassmaking, mathematics and astrology. The last item would develop from their interest in astronomy.

Soothsayers (Gazerim) dealt with astrological phenomena and portents.

Wise Men are thought to include the main categories described above. Some refer to them as "physicians".

CHAPTER 2: APPENDIX II

Critics' Views of the Four Empires

The various critics who contend that Daniel's account of Nebuchadnezzar's dream originated in the Maccabaean period, have divided each of the first three of these powers into two, in order to make four by that time in the world's history; but that will not do. The Assyrian is not in the picture. The dream clearly starts with Babylon. The Medo-Persian power comfortably fits the two arms, the one being slightly more powerful than the other as in normal humanity. The Medes and Persians did not rule as successive world-wide powers, but jointly under one headship. Nor can the divided state which succeeded Alexander the Great, be represented as a Greek fourth power. The details given in Daniel 7 of the parallel vision of Daniel, of the third and fourth beasts, exclude this interpretation. The stone falls upon the fourth metal's divided state, and that certainly did not happen in Greek times.

CHAPTER 2: APPENDIX III

"The God of Heaven"

When the Chaldeans are unable to reveal Nebuchadnezzar's dream, they say (verse 11), "No one can reveal it to the king except the gods, and they do not live among men" (N.I.V.). In this statement they use the Aramaic word Elah for god or gods. But so does Daniel when he says, "There is a God in heaven that revealeth secrets" and "the God of heaven maketh known to the king . . ."

Elah is thus the Aramaic abstract title for a god, whether true or false. Nebuchadnezzar was a polytheist, but his principal devotion was to Bel-Merodach. When addressing Nebuchadnezzar, Daniel does not use the Hebrew divine titles to identify *his* God, but refers to Him by His qualities, as "the God of Heaven."

In the parts of the book written in Hebrew, Daniel does use the Hebrew titles for God and Lord, as El, Elohim, Adon, Adonai and Yahweh, especially in chapter 9 which contains his prayer concerning the expiry of the 70 years captivity, and which was answered by the revelation of the 70 'sevens' of years to Messiah the Prince.

CHAPTER 3

THREE main subjects present themselves for consideration in this chapter. First, the image Nebuchadnezzar made; second, Daniel's three friends and their experience in the fiery furnace; and third, the details of the narrative which, in the light of archaeology, dispel the arguments of scepticism. The third item will be found dealt with in Appendix I.

The Image of Gold

Although the events described in chapters 2, 3 and 4 are probably separated by considerable lapses of time, they follow a natural sequence. The dream of chapter 2 flatters Nebuchadnezzar by making him the head of gold, yet indicating his eventual degeneration and overthrow by another (silver) power. Nebuchadnezzar, ignoring this warning, is inflated with pride which expresses itself in the chapter before us. Yet, in spite of the frustration of his self-aggrandisement by the survival of the three friends in the fiery furnace, he persists in his evil way, and has finally to be humbled by God, being reduced to living like an animal (as related in chapter 4).

The episode is undated in Daniel. Can we ascertain when it happened? Some writers suggest that the idea was put into Nebuchadnezzar's mind by the sight of the colossal statues he had seen in Egypt. It appears that during the war with Pharaoh-Necho in 601 B.C. he invaded Egypt, but suffered a defeat, and as a consequence stayed at home in 600 B.C. This invasion would be two years after his dream of the image, so the respite at home would provide an excellent opportunity for his project, a boost to his morale and also that of his officials.

Assuming then that Nebuchadnezzar had already campaigned in Egypt, he could have seen the colossus of Rameses II. We are told that most Egyptian king-images are seated; but there is this notable exception. On the other hand most Assyrian king-images are standing. Must not Nebuchadnezzar's glory, majesty and prestige be expressed in such a way as to exceed this Egyptian marvel?

The size of the image has been questioned: 60 cubits by 6 cubits is an unusual proportion—ten to one—for the dimensions of a man. The height of a tall man might be about four times his width; but if the statue was on a pedestal, we can visualize the possibility of a statue of a man being four times 6 cubits high. If to 24 cubits, we add 6 cubits for head-gear, and a pedestal of 15 cubits in height, on a plinth of 15 cubits, we have a total height of 60 cubits.

The site where the image was erected was in "the plain of Dura in the province of Babylon". *Dur* means Wall, so that the plain in front of the wall would be "the plain of Dura", and what was erected in it would be clearly visible from the city. Moreover there were other Duras in the country, so the detail "in the province of Babylon" is added. There is a plain south-east of Babylon which is still known by that name, in which among other ruins a square mound made of baked bricks has been found, which is 46 feet square and 20 feet high, eminently suitable to be the base of a huge statue. The archaeologists consider this to be the site of the image; and the 20 feet would correspond to the 15 cubits suggested above.[1]

Though golden, the image may not have been *solid*; yet, even today in a temple in Bangkok, there is a solid gold image of the Buddha weighing 5¼ tons. In Nebuchadnezzar's dream only the head was of gold; but in his pride Nebuchadnezzar disregards the limitations of the dream and makes his image *all* of gold. It is probable that this "image" was a statue of Nebuchadnezzar himself, although the text does not explicitly say so; but even so, it would be regarded as the embodiment of his god Merodach. There exists a statue of Shalmaneser III of which he says, "I made an image of my royalty; upon it I inscribed the praise of Assur my master and a true account of my exploits". This seems to reflect the principle of Assyrian potentates, which is thus carried on by Nebuchadnezzar. Clearly the image was to be regarded as an object of worship. As Nebuchadnezzar had worshipped Daniel as the embodiment of *his* God, who could reveal the dream, so he evidently expected his people to worship *him* as the embodiment of Bel-Merodach.

The Babylonians, like a number of other ancient nations, were fond of music, so that was used as the signal for the moment of dedication, by causing all worshippers to prostrate themselves in worship. The instruments employed are considered in the Appendix. We pass now to look at the reaction of the three friends of Daniel to the command of Nebuchadnezzar to worship the image, and the threatened punishment for disobedience.

1. J. Urquhart, *The Inspiration and Accuracy of the Holy Scripture*, p. 417

The Fiery Furnace

The barbaric practice used as a threat to ensure obedience to Nebuchadnezzar's orders, was not an uncommon one. There are other instances recorded in inscriptions. The "furnace" was probably a brick-baking kiln. Some such have been found, built like a railway tunnel open at one end, so that Nebuchadnezzar could see what was going on inside. The heating seven times hotter than usual could hardly be taken literally, but is an instance of the Babylonians using the number seven as the Hebrews did, as a symbol of completeness.

Shadrach, Meshach and Abednego were denounced by the "Chaldeans", or astrologers, for disobeying Nebuchadnezzar's orders, which illustrates the jealousy of these officials that smouldered beneath the surface. The word for "accused" signifies a persistent malice and craft. By informing Nebuchadnezzar, the Chaldeans calumniated and slandered the three Jews. Literally, the word says "they ate them up". Shadrach, Meshach and Abednego owed their exalted station to Nebuchadnezzar's favour. Their obvious duty was to show him respect; their attitude therefore would appear to him to be the height of ingratitude, as well as a profane and irreligious act—hence his rage and fury. It is said that the original word is stronger even than that of Daniel 2:12, and implies a "passion and glowing anger".

Nebuchadnezzar's words in verse 15, "And who is that God that shall deliver you out of my hands?", reflect the defiant attitude of Sennacherib (2 Kings 18:35) and of Pharaoh (Exodus 5:2). Even if the statue had been a statue of Nebuchadnezzar, it also stood for his god Merodach. From Nebuchadnezzar's point of view his 'god' had given him conquest over Judah, and for his captives to refuse worship was the extreme insult. Yet, from their point of view, it would have been pure idolatry. Shadrach, Meshach and Abednego say in effect, "We need not answer you, God will answer you" (3:14-18). God was their confidence; they had eyes of faith. The three friends had the assurance of God through Isaiah, "When thou passest through the waters, I will be with thee; and through the rivers, they shall not overflow thee: when thou walkest through the fire, thou shalt not be burned; neither shall the flame kindle upon thee" (43:2). Perhaps they remembered Elisha being surrounded by horses and chariots of fire when the Syrians set out to capture him (2 Kings 6:17). The God of Israel had more control over fire than the Babylonians. "Our God is a consuming fire" (Deuteronomy 4:24; 9:3; Hebrews 12:29). God "answered" both

Moses and Elijah "by fire", to consume sacrifices, to destroy rebels, as well as to protect the faithful by the "pillar of fire".

Noah was protected and saved by the same element that destroyed the world. Lot was taken away from the fire of Sodom. In the future conflagration we too may be taken away, or possibly preserved in some such way as the three friends, or as was Israel at the Red Sea. Enemies are always trying to undermine the faithful. The Chaldeans tried to trap the three friends; later they trapped Daniel in the den of lions. The victims relied upon God, and God *did* deliver them, but they did not *presume* on it. They *believed* God was well able to deliver them. So it should be with us: whenever we are faced with alternatives in danger, we must always adhere to what is *right*. "They that be with us are more than they that be with them", said Elisha. Fire is the Scriptural medium by which to describe the testing of a man's faith. "If need be, ye are in heaviness through manifold temptations (trials): that the trial of your faith, being much more precious than of gold that perisheth, though it be tried with fire, might be found unto praise and honour and glory at the appearing of Jesus Christ" (1 Peter 1:6,7; also 1 Corinthians 3:10-15).

The three friends having been bound and thrown into the fire, Nebuchadnezzar is astonished to see four men walking freely and safely in the midst of the fire, and the fourth is "like a son of the gods" (verses 20-25). In verse 28 he describes the fourth figure as an angel, or messenger. Nebuchadnezzar uses the word *bar:* bar-elohim. In his religion Iz-bar is the god of fire. As a result of God's intervention, the fire has no power, and the three are recalled by Nebuchadnezzar, who then characteristically goes to the opposite extreme: Shadrach, Meshach and Abednego are promoted, and the Chaldeans are thwarted.

Since the text offers no explanation for Daniel being uninvolved in this incident, it is idle to speculate. It may however be observed, that "truth is stranger than fiction", and that no writer given to romancing would have omitted his principal hero from such a narrative, had he been present.

CHAPTER 3: APPENDIX I

The Detail in the Narrative

Titles: Verses 2 and 3 mention the following ranks of officials: "Princes, governors, captains, judges, treasurers, counsellors, sheriffs, rulers of provinces". Some modern versions substitute other words for some of these titles, but the original words are all genuine Assyrian titles found in documents of Nineveh and Babylon.

The "herald" of verse 4 (*karoza*), has been seized upon as being a Greek term, but though there is a similar Greek word, the word used here is Semitic and has been found in Assyrian and Babylonian inscriptions with the sense of *edict*.[1]

The clothing worn by the three friends: The meaning of the words describing this was not well understood when the A.V. was translated. The original words are now rendered as follows:

Coats   *sarbalehon*—mantles, long robes;
Hosen   *parishehon*—head covering or decoration;
Hats   *karbehlathon*—undergarment or tunic, kept close to
              the body by a girdle or belt.

These are matters in regard to which a late writer could go wrong. It appears that even when the LXX was translated, the writers did not know what to make of the words, and translated *sarbalehon* in one verse by *hypodemata* (sandals), and in another verse by *sarabara* (loose Persian trousers).

Musical Instruments: The critics used to claim that these were all Greek words and so were proof of a late date for the book. Even if they were all Greek, the conclusion drawn does not follow; but it now appears that only one or two are Greek in origin. The doubtful meaning of some of them is reflected in the translation given in *Speaker's Commentary* which reads, "At what time you hear the sound of the horn, flute?, lyre, triangular harp?, harp?, drum? and all kinds of music, you shall fall down and worship"—four question marks! The

---

1. J. Urquhart, *The Inspiration and Accuracy of the Holy Scripture*, pp. 444-445

words as translated in the A.V. can be briefly summarized as follows, but there is still considerable doubt about what instrument meant:

Cornet: *qeren*—probably a horn (Hebrew or Akkadian in origin);

Flute: *masroqi*—flute or double pipe (Hebrew);

Harp: *qayteros*—lyre—LXX *kithara* (a loan word to Hebrew and Greek);

Sackbut: *sabk*—LXX *sambuke*—a 4-stringed triangular harp (possibly an Aramaic loan word);

Psaltery: *pesanterin*—a stringed instrument of triangular shape (borrowed from Greek);

Dulcimer: *sumphoneya*—possibly a bagpipe or a tympanon (borrowed from Greek, or it may mean "all the foregoing played in unison").

Archaeological and historical discoveries show there is nothing strange in signs of Greek words appearing in the book of Daniel, supposing it to have been written in his own lifetime. Points that have been made to show early intercommunication between Greece and Assyria, Babylonia and other countries, may be summarised as follows:

(i) Greek statesmen in trouble in their own cities, are known to have fled to Persia long before the birth of Alexander the Great.

(ii) Flinders Petrie discovered two Greek cities in Egypt (Naukratis and Daphne; the latter is Tahpanhes), which accommodated 30,000 Greek troops about 665 B.C. Jews were in contact with Egypt at that time, so that Greek musical instruments could well have been seen in Solomon's Temple.

(iii) Ancient Greek commerce with Tyre and places further east is referred to in Ezekiel 27:4,13,23; Greeks even used a Hebrew or Phoenician word to designate gold.

(iv) The name of a commodity travels with it; many instances of this occur at the present time, with such well-known commodies as tea, sugar, coffee, muslin etc.

(v) The ancient name of Greece, Javan, occurs in inscriptions of Sargon (Assyrian); they also depict bands of men and women dancing, singing, playing harp, viols, tabor and pipe.

(vi) Musical instruments were the customary accompaniment of triumphal processions.

(vii) A relief of Ashurbanipal from Nineveh shows two musicians together, one with an eight-string, and one with a five-string lyre.

(viii) The sackbut, or four-string triangular harp, was usually played horizontally; a number of these appear on Assyrian reliefs.

(ix) For perhaps the most telling evidence of all, we will quote the words of John Urquhart: "We have the most positive proof that one Greek instrument at least got to Nineveh some 40 or 50 years before Nebuchadnezzar began to reign. The *cithera* (or harp), with seven strings, was invented by Terpander, a Greek musician and poet, about 650 B.C. This event and date are fixed by Greek testimony. But the same seven-stringed harp is sculptured upon a monument erected by Ashurbanipal, king of Assyria, about this very time. 'This invention', says M. Lenormant, 'is ascribed to Terpander about 650 B.C.; and on the Assyrian monuments this *cithera* with seven strings appears only from the time of Ashurbanipal (668-625). The coincidence of these dates' he adds, 'is striking' ... No time was lost in carrying Terpander's invention to the Assyrian court.' This proves that an enterprising commerce was at that time in full activity between Assyria and Greece, and that Greek musical instruments were purchased and valued by Assyrians and Babylonians before the time of Daniel.''[2]

---

2. J. Urquhart, *The Inspiration and Accuracy of the Holy Scriptures*, pp. 425,434-435; also see T. C. Mitchell, *Notes on some Problems in the Book of Daniel*, pp. 19-27 regarding musical instruments.

CHAPTER 4

ONCE again, Nebuchadnezzar's sleep is disturbed, and again the various orders of wise men are called in to allay his fears and anxiety. Yet again the wise men are completely at a loss to interpret the meaning of the dream. Belteshazzar (Daniel) is "master of the magicians", so presumably too important an individual to be involved unless all else fails, but he is appealed to eventually.

The Dream of the Tree

In explaining to Daniel, the king refers to the "watchers" and "holy ones" appearing in the dream, and attributes Daniel's power to interpret dreams to "the spirit of the holy gods" being in him. No doubt his choice of words reflects his conception of these manifestations in terms of his pagan polytheistic beliefs; yet he states the truth for the revelation of which the dream is given. Daniel, for his part, describes the purport of the dream as being the *decree of the most High*. Nebuchadnezzar might have deduced the principle of this lesson from his earlier dream (chapter 2); but his pride had blinded his eyes, and even the events of chapter 3 have not sufficiently humbled him. God graciously grants him another dream, and reveals through him to the rest of *mankind*, a knowledge of His will and purpose, and His approval of a spirit of humility. "What doth the Lord require of thee, but to do justly, and to love mercy, and to walk humbly with thy God?" (Micah 6:8).

The whole of chapter 4 consists of Nebuchadnezzar's account of the incident, in order to confess and renounce his pride. By any standard it is a remarkable experience and a remarkable statement, unlikely to be parallelled in secular history. In the dream, Nebuchadnezzar is represented by a tree, high, strong, fair, fruitful and visible world-wide. The tree is not an uncommon representation of nations in Scripture. In Ezekiel 31:3 we read: "Behold, the Assyrian was a cedar in Lebanon with fair branches." In the dream the tree is to be hewn down, and seven times are to pass over it. Times are measured in days, weeks, months or years. These particular "times" or "seasons" are usually accepted to mean years, though the text does not specify the length of a "time". In his description Nebuchadnezzar speaks in the first person, except where his madness is being described, which is appropriately related in the third person, as he was then incapable. The tree is described as having a man's heart which is exchanged for the heart of a beast, and it is decreed: "*Let seven times pass over him.*" The object of the dream is given in verse 17: "To the intent that the living may know that the most High ruleth in the kingdom of men, and giveth it to whomsoever he will, and setteth up over it the basest of men."

Daniel's interpretation comes in verses 25-26:

"They shall drive thee from men, and thy dwelling shall be with the beasts of the field, and they shall make thee to eat grass as oxen, and they shall wet thee with the dew of heaven, and seven times shall pass over thee, till thou know that the most High ruleth in the kingdom of men, and giveth it to whomsoever he will. And whereas they commanded to leave the stump of the tree roots; thy kingdom shall be sure unto thee, after that thou shalt have known that the heavens do rule."

Then follows the exhortation addressed to Nebuchadnezzar by Daniel (verse 27):

"Wherefore, O king, let my counsel be acceptable unto thee, and break off thy sins by righteousness, and thine iniquities by shewing mercy to the poor; if it may be a lengthening of thy tranquillity."

Daniel was bold indeed to address such a man in such a way; but though the advice seems to have been taken in good part by the king, he appears to have ignored it; for one year later he was again boasting about "this great Babylon, that I have built for the house of the kingdom by the might of my power, and for the honour of my majesty" (verse 30). Then the blow falls and "he was driven from men, and did eat grass as oxen" (verse 33). This humiliating form of illness, although of infrequent occurrence, is well-known in the medical profession and used at one time to be called lycanthropy.

At the end of the "times" Nebuchadnezzar "lifted up his eyes", and his understanding returned to him (verses 34-35):

"I blessed the most High, and I praised and honoured him that liveth for ever, whose dominion is an everlasting dominion, and his kingdom is from generation to generation: and all the inhabitants of the earth are reputed as nothing: and he doeth according to his will in the army of heaven, and among the inhabitants of the earth: and none can stay his hand, or say unto him, What doest thou?"

When Nebuchadnezzar's reason returned to him, he continued:

"I was established in my kingdom, and excellent majesty was added unto me. Now I Nebuchadnezzar praise and extol and honour the King of heaven, all whose works are truth, and his ways judgment: and those that walk in pride he is able to abase" (verses 36,37).

Some take this expression of praise to mean that as a result of his experience Nebuchadnezzar was converted to a belief in the God of Israel, but others doubt it. "How deeply the lesson went is open to question, for characteristic self-centred language reappears ... This impersonal reference to God keeps Him at a distance, and this last word of Nebuchadnezzar in the book, while formally acknowledging the power and justice of God, appears to fall short of penitence and true faith".[1] The vital question surely is: Did the experience detach Nebuchadnezzar from his adoration of Bel-Merodach? There is nothing in the text to suggest that it did. The claims of the God of Israel are exclusive; He cannot be regarded as just another addition to the pantheon, however superior.

The important principle taught by the dream, and thus acknowledged by Nebuchadnezzar in verse 17, is that "the most High ruleth in the kingdom of men, and giveth it to whomsoever he will, and setteth up over it the basest of men". Although God may permit 'base' men, such as Hitler, to rule, the original word for *base* is here said to mean, literally, the low and humble ones in rank and esteem, rather than the ignoble in character. Daniel understood this and pressed the point upon the attention of Nebuchadnezzar (verses 25-27), so that even Nebuchadnezzar might continue to rule if he would be humble.

Some see in this expression "the basest of men", a reference to the origins of Nebuchadnezzar's father, Nabopolassar. It is said that in one of his inscriptions he describes himself as the "son of a nobody". The phrase "son of a nobody" has also been applied in an inscription to Hazael king of Syria, with the meaning that he was a usurper.[2] This may be the meaning to apply to Nabopolassar, because he founded the Chaldean dynasty of Babylon, and may not detract from the high standing with the Chaldean tribe which some attribute to him.

Taken as a prophecy, this may be regarded as a Messianic passage, after the manner of 2 Samuel 23:3, "He that ruleth over men must be

---

1. J. G. Baldwin, *Daniel*, Tyndale Commentaries, I.V.P., p. 116
2. *New Bible Dictionary*, I.V.P., p. 507

just, ruling in the fear of God''. The late J. W. Thirtle, in addition to making the point of the previous paragraph, writes, ''The divine purpose is to *set up* a particular king. While he suffers others to sit on their thrones and exercise authority, He does not *establish* them there. The Deity will not exalt the vile and good-for-nothing; but He does purpose exalting the lowly, the humble, the rejected of men. It is not surprising, then, to find that in the original Chaldee of this verse, we have a reference to *one person*, and we must render: 'the lowest (one) of men He will set over it'. There is a distinct allusion to the lowliest, the most humble, the least esteemed, the least regarded of all men; and we know that this one is he who will be exalted (Isaiah 52 and 53). We read here that the Deity giveth the kingdom to 'whomsoever he will', and in Ezekiel 21:27, that it will be given to him 'whose right it is', in which latter place it is written: 'Exalt him that is low, and make him low that is exalted ... ' ''[3]

The dream of chapter 4 thus underlines that of chapter 2 in emphasising the fact that God is in control of the kingdoms of men, and together they are intended to impress the fact upon the minds of *men*.

The principle of extending the symbol of the golden head beyond Nebuchadnezzar himself, as exemplified in chapter 2, also applies to chapter 4 in which he records the second dream. The historical data of Nebuchadnezzar's reign outside Scripture is meagre; it is not easy to allocate precisely the seven years of his madness, yet we might well ask whether a dream of such great detail is intended to teach a moral lesson and nothing more? No political disturbance seems to have arisen from his madness; and if it occurred after his invasion of Egypt in his 37th year, it seems that he could only have been restored to his throne about one year before he died. Several Babylonian kings followed Nebuchadnezzar on the throne, yet the next account is of the overthrow of the whole kingdom by Darius the Mede. Does not this fact significantly link the hewing down of the Tree with the fall of Babylon? Thus the Babylonian supremacy of seven decades of years continued until 538-536 B.C., when the Imperial tree was cut down by Cyrus.

The very vagueness of the phrase ''seven times'' strongly suggests a symbolic period, literal periods usually being expressed in so many years and months. (Although the possibility of the phrase meaning seven years of years, i.e. 365 × 7, should not be discounted.) This

3. J. W. Thirtle, *The Christadelphian*, 1882, p. 543; see also *Speaker's Commentary* on Daniel 4:17

being so, seven times pass over the tree stump, and in the imperial sense madness overtakes the kingdoms of men for whatever time is involved. "All the nations, to whom I send thee . . . shall be moved, and be mad" (Jeremiah 25:15,16); "Babylon hath been a golden cup in the Lord's hand . . . the nations have drunken of her wine; therefore the nations are mad" (51:7). In fact, in this very context Jeremiah draws a parallel between the overthrow of Babylon, and the ending of the kingdoms of men. Daniel realised that the accession of Darius marked the fulfilment of the 70 years of captivity foretold by Jeremiah. Although Israel and the surrounding nations were to drink the cup of the Lord's fury, that affliction was limited to 70 years; and then "the king of Sheshach (Babylon) shall drink after them" (25:26). The latter part of the prophecy, however, cannot possibly be limited to what took place in the days of Cyrus, because it involves many nations, or "all flesh". Jeremiah continues:

"I will call for a sword upon all the inhabitants of the earth . . . the Lord shall roar from on high, and utter his voice from his holy habitation . . . The Lord hath a controversy with the nations, he will plead with all flesh . . . evil shall go forth from nation to nation, and a great whirlwind shall be raised up from the coasts of the earth. And the slain of the Lord shall be at that day from one end of the earth even unto the other end of the earth: they shall not be lamented, neither gathered, nor buried; they shall be dung upon the ground" (Jeremiah 25:29-33).

This is an event of world-wide proportions, much greater than the overthrow of Babylon; but the prophecy makes the fall of Babylon by which a State of Israel was restored, typical of the final controversy which will result in the establishment of the Kingdom of God.

In view of this parallel, can we apply "seven times" to the stump of the kingdoms of men? and if so, how? First, we must consider the principles upon which this may be done. In Nebuchadnezzar's Image dream, he is only the head; and it is quite obvious that what was "to come to pass hereafter" is represented by the rest of the detail right up to the supplanting of the kingdoms of men by the Kingdom of God. Is it not reasonable to interpret the Tree dream in a similar manner, and to regard the new time factor which is introduced as a definition of the length of time that the stump of the kingdoms of men will remain bound and rooted in the earth?

The principle of "a day for a year" interpretation is discussed in the appendix to this chapter. Granted this, we must enquire when the seven times start. Disappointment caused by premature anticipations already expired, has rather thrust this subject into the background. The disappointment arises because earlier interpreters have started counting from too early a date. Faber takes his start with the *birth* of Nebuchadnezzar. Dr. Guinness counted from the political *rise* of Nebuchadnezzar, i.e. his capture of Jerusalem. Dr. John Thomas also started from this same point.[4]

But, in the dream it is the *Babylonian* Tree that is cut down, not the Judaic, and that happened ca. 538-536 B.C. The inference is that the time period starts from this *point of action* in the vision. It must be admitted that this suggestion does not completely eliminate the problems created by the use of earlier starting points, for 2520 years from 538/6 B.C. brings us to 1983/5. As this period has expired without an important terminal event, we must conclude that the starting date has still not been correctly identified; or that the period should be calculated on the basis of solar years (this would extend the period another 36 or 37 years); or that, like Nebuchadnezzar himself, the kingdoms of men will continue for an undefined period of time after the expiry of the seven "times" allocated for their supremacy.

---

4. Faber, *The Sacred Calendar*, Vol. II, p. 37 (1828)
   H. Grattan Guinness, *The Approaching End of the Age*, pp. 294-326, 371
   J. Thomas, *Exposition of Daniel*, pp. 111-112

CHAPTER 4: APPENDIX I

A Day for a Year

The only principle for the calculation of long prophetic periods contained in Scripture is what is known as the "day-for-a-year" principle. The precedent is derived from the Exodus and the occasion when Ezekiel had to lie on his side (Numbers 14:34; Ezekiel 4:4-6), and is supported by the fulfilment of the 70 weeks prophecy, with the cutting off of Messiah about 490 years from a decree connected with the rebuilding of Jerusalem (Daniel 9:24). There is, however, much more to it than this. A fairly detailed survey of the arguments for the justification of the day-for-a-year principle may be found in *The Approaching End of the Age* by Dr. H. Grattan Guinness (10th Ed., 1886, pp. 293-322), of which the following is but a brief summary.

Where it is necessary for Scripture to mention a period of time, even prophetically, it quotes the period *literally*: as, for example, 400 years for the pilgrimage of Abraham and his descendants. There are other instances (Genesis 6:3; 15:13; Numbers 14:34; Isaiah 23:15; Jeremiah 25:11). Other predictions are made with the dual object of revealing the future but concealing the time from early generations. God's foreknowledge is a great comfort to believers, and it is His will to reveal events to them without necessarily revealing their duration. He therefore uses mysterious symbolic forms; hiding from one generation, but revealing to another. The duration assigned may partly determine what the symbols themselves mean.

As a map is drawn to a miniature but uniform scale, so these symbols are hieroglyphs representative of powers, but the time factors have to be given in words, also proportionately on a reduced scale. The 70 weeks prophecy supplies the key to the rest. The "futurist" view which seeks to insist that all these vaguely expressed periods be taken literally, originally did so to evade the identification of certain prophecies with the Papacy; the idea has since been taken over by Protestants, but to do this "makes a mystery without a meaning". Dr. Grattan Guinness summarises a lengthy exposition on the subject by Professor Birks, and argues that the liveliness of our expectation of the Lord's speedy return

41

depends upon our judgement of the true meaning of the statements of time in symbolic chronological prophecy. Birks says that the rejection of prophetic chronology which follows a denial of the year-day system of interpretation "is most of all to be deplored from its deadly and paralysing influence on the great hope of the church. No delusion can be greater than to expect, by excluding all reference to time and dates, to awaken Christians to a more lively expectation of their Lord's second coming . . . Every sign of the times is either too vague to direct us, or in proportion as it becomes distinct, assumes practically all the characters of a numerical date, and becomes exposed to the same objections . . . The prophetic times indeed, when separated from the context . . . are a dry and worthless skeleton, but when taken in connection with the related events, clothed with historical facts, and joined with those spiritual affections . . . give strength to what was feeble . . . form and beauty and order, to the whole outline and substance of these sacred and Divine prophecies".[1]

Birks sums up the "year-day theory" in the following maxims:

1. That after the ascension of Christ the church was intended by God to be kept in the lively expectation of his speedy return in glory.

2. That in the Divine counsels a long period, of nearly two thousand years, was to intervene between the first and the second advent; and to be marked by a dispensation of grace to the Gentiles.

3. That in order to strengthen the faith and hope of the church under the long delay, a large part of the whole interval was prophetically announced, but in such a manner that its true length might not be understood, until its own close seemed to be drawing near.

4. That in the symbolic prophecies of Daniel and John, other "times" were also revealed, and included under one common maxim of interpretation.

5. That the periods thus figuratively revealed are exclusively those of Daniel and John, which relate to the general history of the church, between the time of the prophet and the second advent.

6. That in these predictions each day represents a natural year, as in the vision of Ezekiel; that a month denotes thirty, and a "time" or "year" three hundred and sixty years.[2]

---

1. H. G. Guinness, *The Approaching End of the Age*, pp. 297-8, quoting T. R. Birks, *Elements of Sacred Prophecy*, p. 415
2. Ibid., p. 305

"The year-day theory rests on a surprising combination of Scriptural arguments . . . First of all there are four or five distinct presumptions of a general kind, that the dates have some secret meaning. There are, then, three plain and certain, and one more disputable passage, which supply an express *rule of interpretation*, and *a key* at once simple and comprehensive, the direct appointment of God Himself. When we further proceed to examine the passages in detail, we find that every one, without exception, yields some peculiar argument, in support of this same view; and several of them furnish us with two or three distinct proofs".[3]

Accepting the foregoing in principle, we pass to the application. The Babylonian and Hebrew calendars were lunar and therefore contained 354 days in the year. This necessitated the insertion of intercalary months to bring the calendar into line with the seasons, which of course are solar. Our western calendar consisting of 365 days is an attempt to adopt a solar measurement, but even then there remain awkward fractions to be accounted for. There, is however, a Scriptural procedure for counting 360 days for the year, since the symbolic periods of "42 months", "1260 days" and "time, times and half a time" are equated in certain passages.

In Revelation 11:2,3, 42 months are equated with 1260 days; and in chapter 12:6,14, 3½ times are equated with 1260 days. Therefore the same expression in Daniel 7:25 and 12:7 must have the same value:

$$42 \times 30 = 1260$$

$$1260/3\frac{1}{2} = 360$$

$$12 \times 30 = 360$$

If one "time" = 360 days
then 7 times = 2520 day-years

---

3. Ibid. p. 322

CHAPTER 5

IN this chapter the narrative passes from the reign of Nebuchad-nezzar to the very end of the Babylonian Empire under Belshazzar, ignoring all that happened in between. As previously remarked, this suggests that from the point of view of symbolism, on a larger view, the Golden Headship of Nebuchadnezzar and his experiences stood for the whole Empire, and also applied to the headship of all the kingdoms of men.

Belshazzar's Feast

The scene before us is of a feast and the drinking of wine. We are not told how long it lasted, but to his carousing Belshazzar added an arrogant sacrilege which it would appear none of the previous kings had ever dared to commit. He commanded the holy vessels captured by king Nebuchadnezzar from God's temple in Jerusalem, to be brought in and used for his debauchery; "and the king, and his princes, his wives, and his concubines, drank in them. They drank wine, and praised gods of gold, and of silver, of brass, of iron, of wood, and of stone" (verses 3,4).

This was a deliberate decision, which was an affront, even a challenge to Yahweh, the God of Israel. It was no casual accident; he *sent* for them, and it took time for them to be brought and distributed between his princes, wives and concubines. They then drank their wine from them.

The Writing on the Wall

It is at this point that God intervened, and the mysterious "part of a hand" wrote the famous words on the plaster of the wall. We are not informed what the writing was, until Daniel arrived to interpret it. Although what follows in the Biblical record takes only a few minutes to read, the fear and consternation among the revellers must have been considerable. Only the reaction of Belshazzar is described; maybe he was the only one to see the writing actually happening: "The king's countenance was changed, and his thoughts troubled him, so that the joints of his loins were loosed, and his knees smote one against another'' (verse 6). However, the words remained on the wall and, as Nebuchadnezzar had done before him, Belshazzar sent for the "astrologers, the Chaldeans, and the soothsayers" to explain them; but, as usual, they failed to provide a solution. It is unlikely that they were unable to read the actual words, which were in Aramaic, but their implication eluded them. All this must have taken some time, during which Belshazzar was doubtless getting more and more agitated. He was "greatly troubled, and his countenance was changed in him, and his lords were astonied" (verse 9).

A woman comes to the rescue. "The queen . . . came into the banquet house." As Belshazzar's wives were already present, this must mean the wife of Nabonidus, Belshazzar's mother. Probably she was a daughter of Nebuchadnezzar, and a strong personality. She, hearing of the hubbub, entered unbidden, and advised Belshazzar to send for Daniel of whom she evidently knew a great deal. She related the high reputation Daniel had in the days of Nebuchadnezzar: "Forasmuch as an excellent spirit, and knowledge, and understanding, interpreting of dreams, and shewing of hard sentences, and dissolving of doubts, were found in the same Daniel, whom the king named Belteshazzar" (verse 12).

Daniel was therefore sent for, and Belshazzar, having recovered some degree of equanimity, assumed an official manner, checked the origin and reputation of Daniel, and confessed the inability of his "wise men" to interpret the writing. He concluded: "If thou canst read the writing, and make known to me the interpretation thereof, thou shalt be clothed with scarlet, and have a chain of gold about thy neck, and shalt be the third ruler in the kingdom" (verse 16).

In majestic words Daniel openly rebuked Belshazzar: "Let thy gifts be to thyself, and give thy rewards to another; yet I will read the writing unto the king, and make known to him the interpretation" (verse 17). After reminding Belshazzar of the humbling of Nebuchadnezzar, Daniel continued:

"And thou his son, O Belshazzar, hast not humbled thine heart, though thou knewest all this; but hast lifted up thyself against the Lord of heaven; and they have brought the vessels of his house before thee, and thou, and thy lords, thy wives, and thy concubines, have drunk wine in them; and thou hast praised the gods of silver and gold . . . which see not, nor hear, nor know: and the God in whose hand thy breath is, and whose are all thy ways, hast thou not glorified: then

was the part of the hand sent from him; and this writing was written:
MENE, MENE, TEKEL, UPHARSIN'' (verses 22-25).

The writing was then interpreted by Daniel. The four words are the names of weights, which being standardised were sometimes used as currency. At least one example has been found with the word stamped upon it.[1] The words written on the wall were in Aramaic, and the nouns they represent are given by Daniel the meaning of the roots from which they are derived.

Mene: mina or maneh, means *numbered* or appointed.[2]

Tekel: shekel, and means *weighed* or assessed (1 Samuel 2:3).

Upharsin: The *U* means 'and'; *parsin* is plural, meaning halves or parts; thus

Peres: half or part of a maneh, and verbally, shared or *divided*.[3]

By an additional play upon the word, Daniel took the consonantal form P R S, and changing the vowel pointing to PaRaS, interpreted it as "divided and given to the (Medes and) Persians".

The interpretation is, "God hath *numbered* thy kingdom, and finished it; thou art *weighed* in the balances, and art found wanting; thy kingdom is *divided*, and given to the Medes and Persians".

Despite the adverse interpretation, Daniel was rewarded in the way Belshazzar promised and made third ruler in the kingdom. Here again is an undesigned harmony of the book with the facts. Nabonidus was king, but absent from the city; as his regent, Belshazzar was in second place; the third place was the greatest gift at his disposal to bestow upon Daniel.

The narrative concludes abruptly with the information that, "In that night was Belshazzar the king of the Chaldeans slain, and Darius the Median took the kingdom, being about threescore and two years old"

---

1. J. G. Baldwin, *Daniel*, Tyndale Commentaries, I.V.P., p. 123
2. Translated "pound" in A.V. 1 Kings 10:17; Ezra 2:69; Nehemiah 7:71-72; and translated "set" in A.V. Daniel 2:49; 3:12
3. On the basis of Ezekiel 45:12, a numerical value has been given to these terms, thus 20 gerahs = 1 shekel; 50 shekels = 1 mina. Therefore 1 mina = 1000 gerahs (twice), 1 shekel = 20 gerahs, a half-mina = 500 gerahs, totalling 2520 gerahs, thus corresponding with the number of years in seven times. However, there appears to be some uncertainty about the value of a mina or maneh

The death of Belshazzar thus left Daniel, aged as he was, as the highest authority in the city, and presumably co-operative with Darius, as his representative.

We know that Cyrus had been besieging the city for about two years. Doubtless Belshazzar regarded it as impregnable: hence his bravado in calling for the feast. However, though Jeremiah had prophesied the supremacy of Babylon for 70 years (Jeremiah 25:12), he had also in the same verse pronounced its doom; later, he forecast also the manner of it:

"One post shall run to meet another, and one messenger to meet another, to shew the king of Babylon that his city is taken at one end, and that the passages are stopped, and the reeds they have burned with fire, and the men of war are affrighted... I will dry up her sea, and make her springs dry, and Babylon shall become heaps ..." (Jeremiah 51:31-37).

So it came to pass: Cyrus determined to overthrow Babylon by diverting the river, one of its supposed defences, but he chose to await an opportune occasion, a great feast day when Belshazzar decided to give way to his dissoluteness, and so Cyrus caught everyone off their guard.

A Lesson for Our Days

As we survey the world around us, it is obvious that the event we have been considering has a lesson for the present day. So apt is the phrase, enigmatic though it is, that it is said proverbially of any deteriorating situation that "the writing is on the wall".

Apart from the knowledge that the "times" of Daniel are running out, the words of Jesus, "Upon the earth distress of nations, with perplexity; the sea and the waves roaring; men's hearts failing them for fear; and for looking after those things which are coming on the earth" (Luke 21:25,26), are more pregnant with meaning than they have ever been before.

The world, being a lover of pleasure more than a lover of God, drowns its worries with drink and drugs; views its coming disintegration with a befuddled mind, and finds 'no way out'. It has been weighed in the balance and found wanting; but its kingdom will be given to a greater Messiah than Cyrus (Isaiah 45:1), even Jesus Christ, the King of Kings, and to his saints. How appropriate that the symbolic "Anointed One" should overthrow the symbolic head of the kingdoms of men!

CHAPTER 5: APPENDIX I

Belshazzar and the Inscriptions

There were several short reigns between those of Nebuchadnezzar and Belshazzar which are not mentioned in the book of Daniel. At one time the very existence of Belshazzar himself was denied, on the grounds that the name was unknown *outside* the Bible. However, this name has since been found on a number of inscriptions. The first to be discovered was a group of four cylinders found at the corners of the temple of the Moon-god at Mukayyar (Ur). They are on display at the British Museum, and are inscribed with an account of Nabonidus' rebuilding of that temple, and a prayer to the Moon god Sin, on behalf of himself and his eldest son Bel-shar-usur, who is the Biblical Belshazzar.[1]

The discovery of these tablets was made by Sir Henry Rawlinson in 1854. Since that time other tablets have been found at Hillah, a part of ancient Babylon, which J. Urquhart tells us were bought by Sir Henry for the British Museum in 1876. These were records of a firm of bankers called Sons of Egibi, in some of which Belshazzar is mentioned:

(a) In the 5th year of Nabonidus, the lease of a house is made out to "the secretary of Belshazzar the son of the king".

(b) Six years later, "the sum of 20 manehs of silver for wool, the property of Belshazzar, the son of the king, which has been handed over to Iddin-Nerodach, the son of Basa, the son of Nur-Sin, through the agency of Nabo-Tasabit, the steward of the house of Belshazzar, the son of the king, and the secretaries of the son of the king".[2]

We are also told that Belshazzar "is frequently named on the contract tablets because as crown prince he acted as regent in the absence of his father". Nabonidus "entrusted the kingship to him" and "Belshazzar's name appears associated with that of the king in the oath formulae

---

1. *British Museum Guide to Babylonian & Assyrian Antiquities*, pp. 141-2; illustrated plate 38
2. J. Urquhart, *The Inspiration and Accuracy of the Holy Scripture*, pp. 484-5, 495

of that reign. Since this happened to no other king's son in all Babylonian history, Belshazzar is shown to be king in all but name ..."[3]

---

3. J. G. Baldwin, *Daniel,* Tyndale Commentaries, I.V.P., pp. 21-22

CHAPTER 5: APPENDIX II

Belshazzar: Some Circumstantial Detail

The extravagance of Belshazzar's feast, given for 1000 of his lords, is quite in keeping with the ways of the times. The feast of Ahasuerus, described in the book of Esther, is somewhat later, and on an even larger scale, but it is comparable.

The presence of women at such feasts seems to have been peculiarly characteristic of Babylon, though contrary to the customs of the Persians, Egyptians, and other eastern nations. This fidelity to truth confirms once again the early date of the book. The LXX version, apparently out of deference to contemporary Egyptian susceptibilities, omits reference to the presence of Belshazzar's wives and concubines. Further, the LXX makes no distinction between the names Belshazzar and Belteshazzar (Daniel), evidently having lost already the knowledge that the former name is derived from the god Bel, and the latter from his wife Beltis.[1]

The absence of Nabonidus is accounted for by the fact that he was campaigning against Cyrus by assisting certain kings against whom Cyrus was fighting, such as Croesus king of Lydia, and opposing him as much as possible outside Babylon. A reign of 17 years is attributed to Nabonidus, who seems to have been absent from Babylon for about 10 years. When he heard of the fall of the city he fled to Borsippa; but some writers say that when he eventually surrendered to Cyrus, he was treated mercifully, and given a political appointment, the governorship of Carmania. He was not in the city on the fateful night when Belshazzar was slain.

The relationship between Belshazzar and Nebuchadnezzar has been debated. It seems that he was literally the son of Nabonidus, but the father-son theme seems to be rather laboured in the words of the Queen (5:11), and confirmed by Daniel (in vv. 18,22), which suggests that in order to strengthen his position during the intervening period of intrigue, Nabonidus may have married a daughter of Nebuchadnezzar.

---

1. *Speaker's Commentary*, "Daniel", pp. 299,300

There does not appear to be any reason against Belshazzar being descended from Nebuchadnezzar through his mother. The word "son" is sufficiently imprecise to include grandson, or descendant.[2]

Belshazzar's acquaintance with Daniel: It might appear from a superficial reading of the narrative, that Belshazzar was not previously acquainted with Daniel; but there are several considerations to the contrary:

(i) Daniel 7:1—Daniel's dream of the four beasts took place in the first year of Belshazzar. Owing to the length of the absence of Nabonidus from Babylon noted above, this could have been anything up to 10 years before the fall of the city.

(ii) Daniel 8:1—Daniel's vision of the ram and he goat, took place in the third year of Belshazzar. As a result of this vision he was sick (verse 27), after which he says, "I rose up and did the king's business". Daniel was therefore still in active service in Belshazzar's third year. If it is concluded that Daniel had the vision *in Babylon*, his "business" would have concerned Belshazzar. If he was actually *in Susa* (Shushan the Palace) in Elam when he had the vision, the "business" would probably concern Nabonidus.

(iii) We might conclude that owing to age, Daniel might have been retired some time before the 17th year of Nabonidus, and thus have become out of immediate touch with Belshazzar. It seems that he must have served him for at least some of the time. Obviously Daniel would have had no sympathy with Belshazzar as a personality, nor any wish to attend such a feast.

(iv) Daniel must have known that the end of the kingdom was imminent. The nature of both the dream of chapter 7, and the vision of chapter 8, which had already happened long before Belshazzar held his feast, would have made Daniel well aware of what was in store for the kingdom of Babylon, and we can conclude from 9:1 that he knew that the time when Babylon would fall to the Persians was indeed close at hand.

---

2. J. G. Baldwin, *Daniel,* Tyndale Commentaries, I.V.P., pp. 21-23

CHAPTER 6

WHOEVER Darius the Mede was (see Appendix I), on taking over the kingdom, he soon established friendly relations with Daniel. We are told Darius was 62 years old at that time, and Daniel may well have been approaching 100 (see Chart No. 2). It was obvious Darius would reorganise the government of both the City and the Empire, now entering upon the 'silver' phase represented by the Image. He appointed 120 satraps and three administrators. When he decided to make Daniel the principal of these three and to put him in charge of the whole kingdom, the jealousy of the other men, who were almost certainly much younger than he, was excited, so they conspired to discredit Daniel.

Daniel and the Den of Lions

They rightly considered that it would only be possible to accomplish this on the grounds of his religious differences from them, so they played on the theme of the Eastern concept of the divinity of their rulers. Even until quite recent times this principle was exemplified in the Japanese Emperors. The presidents and princes made representations to the king, and to make it more convincing they involved also the governors, counsellors and captains. They claimed to "have consulted together to establish a royal statute, and to make a firm decree, that whosoever shall ask a petition of any God or man for thirty days, save of thee, O king, he shall be cast into the den of lions. Now, O king, establish the decree, and sign the writing, that it be not changed, according to the law of the Medes and Persians, which altereth not" (verses 7,8).

The flattery of the situation blinded Darius to their duplicity, so he signed the decree. To any Jew it was objectionable, because of the great basic truth of their religion, to which they were witnesses: "The Lord thy God is One Lord, and him only shalt thou serve". When Daniel heard that the writing was signed, he continued to worship as before:

"He went into his house; and his windows being open in his chamber toward Jerusalem, he kneeled upon his knees three times a day, and prayed, and gave thanks before his God, as he did aforetime'' (verse 10).

The men evidently kept watch in order to trap their prey. Verse 11 tells us, ''Then these men assembled, and found Daniel praying and making supplication before his God.'' So they reported him to Darius, emphasising his disregard of the king's authority. It then became clear to Darius that he had been hoodwinked and he made strenuous efforts to release Daniel; but the administrators had another ploy—the principle of the unchangeable nature of Medo-Persian law. So in the end Daniel had to be committed to the den of lions; and Darius extremely reluctantly placed his seal upon it, saying as he did so, ''Thy God whom thou servest continually, he will deliver thee''. It must have been a pathetic sight to behold such an old patriarch, yet such a man of integrity, being treated in this way.

After a sleepless night Darius repaired to the lion's den to find out how Daniel had fared, and was mightily relieved to hear Daniel's reply to his anguished enquiry. Darius spoke with ''a lamentable voice'': ''O Daniel, servant of the Living God, is thy God, whom thou servest continually, able to deliver thee from the lions?'' Daniel replied:

''O king, live forever. My God hath sent his angel, and hath shut the lion's mouths, that they have not hurt me: forasmuch as before him innocency was found in me; and also before thee, O king, have I done no hurt'' (verses 21,22).

Darius was, of course, delighted at this and caused Daniel to be taken out of the den. He then proceeded to wreak vengeance upon the men whose intrigue had placed him in such an embarrassing predicament, and they suffered the fate they had prepared for Daniel.

Like Nebuchadnezzar, Darius records a quite beautiful expression of praise of the God of Daniel:

''I make a decree, That in every dominion of my kingdom men tremble and fear before the God of Daniel: for he is the living God, and stedfast for ever, and his kingdom that which shall not be destroyed, and his dominion shall be even unto the end. He delivereth and rescueth, and he worketh signs and wonders in heaven and in earth, who hath delivered Daniel from the power of the lions'' (verses 26-27).

Note also the point made in verse 23: Daniel was not hurt ''because he believed in his God''. It may be profitable to consider why the other presidents and princes were so determined to get rid of him. His remarks to Darius, that before God "innocency was found in me, and also before thee (Darius) have I done no hurt", may supply the clue. Human nature being what it is, the princes hoped to turn their office to good account by corrupt dealings. They were probably prevented from engaging in such malpractice by the integrity of the man at the top; so they must get rid of him. There is an obvious lesson for our own days, for it is all too easy to be beguiled into involvement in malpractices which have already been collectively agreed upon by one's own colleagues and sanctioned by superiors.

It will be observed that the Medo-Persian conception of God was of a higher order than the Babylonian polytheism. It enabled Darius to describe Daniel's God as *The Living God*, just as faithful Bible characters do. Herein is another textual detail, true for an early date but likely to get confused by a writer in Seleucid times. Just as Nebuchadnezzar represented Bel-Merodach, Darius represented Ormuzd (or Mazda), the Persian god of light and goodness. The Persian concept, however, was not in accord with the revealed religion of Judaism. The Persians contemplated a duality: Ormuzd the god of light was in opposition to Ahriman the god of darkness and evil, much as some moderns believe in a supernatural 'devil' in opposition to God. Appropriately, before Cyrus appeared upon the scene, the prophet Isaiah foretold of him: "Thus saith the Lord to his anointed, to Cyrus, whose right hand I have holden, to subdue nations before him" (45:1). God proceeds to declare repeatedly His unity, "I am the Lord, and there is none else" (verse 5); He cuts across the dual worship of Ormuzd and Ahriman by saying in verse 7, "I form the light, and create darkness: I make peace, and create evil: I the Lord do all these things". There is only *one* Living God. He has control of both light and darkness, and their associations.

Yet, as the apotheosis of Ormuzd, it was up to *Darius* to "shut the mouths of the lions". Daniel seems to imply this when he responds to Darius with the words, "*My* God hath sent his angel and hath shut the lions' mouths, that they have not hurt me." *Speaker's Commentary* remarks: "The most common representative of the evil powers in which the Medo-Persian believed were lions, winged or unwinged. The walls of Persepolis and coins from that period pictured the king— Ormuzd's representative on earth—as the recognised opponent and destroyer of the lions and so of the evil which they symbolized". Nebuchadnezzar was a Babylonian and his method of punishment was a fiery furnace; the Persian method was the den of lions. The book of Daniel gets both right. As had been the case with Shadrach, Meshach and Abednego, who were thrown into the fiery furnace, Daniel was placed in a situation in which it was impossible that he could live without God's intervention. In both cases they were figuratively murdered by men—by *official, governing men*; yet they were delivered by God because of their faith in Him.

Through all the ages of human despotism, believers represent the essential position of witnesses who know God's purpose, and who are under His discipline. God had promised to reveal His purpose to His servants. He controls the despots in spite of themselves, but He also controls His willing servants through their faith and obedience. Their discipline is to be harmless, guileless and innocent; and God's intervention in these cases seems to symbolize a resurrection from an otherwise inevitable death.

Taking place as it does at the beginning of the supremacy of the kingdoms of men over the people of God's covenant, this visible intervention by God on behalf of His servants, first in the early days of their captivity, and then in the early days of their restoration, is particularly significant. As, many centuries afterwards, the words of Jesus and the apostles were "confirmed by signs following", so at the time of Nebuchadnezzar and of Darius God confirmed and underlined the principles He was establishing by dreams and visions, that He *does* rule in the kingdoms of men, no matter how much they *"think not so"* (Isaiah 10:7).

An Application Today?

How about us? Whether we like it or not, whether we realise it or not, we too walk in the midst of 'a den of lions' which could turn on us at any moment—but for the hand of God. God *can* deliver us, but it is not always His will to do so. Whether it be His will or not, we must stand firm as Daniel was prepared to do.

> "Dare to be a Daniel,
> Dare to stand alone;
> Dare to have a purpose firm,
> Dare to make it known".

Let us take to heart the words of Paul to the Thessalonians:

"We ourselves glory in you in the churches of God for your patience and faith in all your persecutions and tribulations that ye endure: which is a manifest token of the righteous judgment of God, that ye may be counted worthy of the kingdom of God, for which ye also suffer: seeing it is a righteous thing with God to recompense tribulation to them that trouble you; and to you who are troubled rest with us, when the Lord Jesus shall be revealed from heaven with his mighty angels, in flaming fire taking vengeance on them that know not God, and that obey not the gospel of our Lord Jesus Christ ... when he shall come to be glorified in his saints, and to be admired in all them that believe ... in that day" (2 Thessalonians 1:4-10).

This sixth chapter concludes the narrative section of the prophecy of Daniel with the remark, "So this Daniel prospered in the reign of Darius and (or, *that is*) in the reign of Cyrus the Persian". Connecting this verse with chapter 1:21 indicates that the career of Daniel extended over the whole period of the captivity; for it was in the first year of Cyrus that he permitted the Jews, and indeed other captive nations as well, to return to the land of their nativity if they so wished (Ezra 1:1-4). It may be that the close intimacy of Daniel with Darius had enabled him to inform Cyrus of the predictions of Isaiah and of Jeremiah, so that he was inspired with the idea of putting them into effect.

CHAPTER 6: APPENDIX I

Darius the Mede

Who was Darius the Mede? Our history books mention three kings by that name; Darius I who was named Hystaspes, was contemporary with the rebuilding of the Temple, at the time of Zerubbabel, Haggai and Zechariah. This is already too late for the Darius in question, so that the others, Darius II Nothus, and Darius III Codomanas, are also out of the question. It has been pointed out, however, that the Persian coin known as a Daric existed before all these and was named after an earlier Darius.

As to who the Darius of Daniel 6 was, there are several theories based on the stories of Herodotus, Xenophon and Ctesius. These men were essentially travellers; and some think they were liable to romance about the enquiries they made in various countries they visited, sometimes long after the events to which they refer took place; and maybe they were somewhat gullible. Their accounts of the matters in hand do not agree, so we cannot be sure of the truth on their authority. It is not worthwhile describing the theories at length. They can be read in the commentaries. The Bible tells us that Darius was a Mede, the son of Ahasuerus (9:1). One theory identifies him with Astyages, son of Cyaxares; another, with Cyaxares II, son of Astyages. The learned say that Cyaxares, Xerxes and Ahasuerus are all forms of the same name, and that these together with Darius, are appellatives and titles of sovereignty like Pharaoh, so that the king in question could only be identified by knowledge of his other name.

Another theory connects Darius with the leader of the army that actually invaded Babylon, who is known as Gobryas; his name on the inscriptions appears as Gubaru. He was made governor of Babylon and the surrounding district by Cyrus, but it appears that "there is no evidence that Gubaru was a Mede, called king, named Darius, a son of Ahasuerus, or aged about sixty".

Yet another theory, which has a distinct appeal, is that advanced by Professor D. J. Wiseman, that Darius was none other than Cyrus himself. History tells us that Cyrus was originally king of Anshan (the

57

same as Elam), the son of Cambyses, an Achaemenian. It appears that either Cambyses or Cyrus married into the Median royal family, thus by a stroke of diplomacy uniting the Median and Persian royal houses. In any case, both nations were of closely kindred blood.

This theory, connecting Darius with Cyrus, was put forward by Professor Wiseman in 1957, and is based on the fact that in Daniel 6:28, the original word for "and" can be understood to mean "even", or "that is"; in fact the N.I.V. gives the latter rendering as an alternative in the margin. In that case the passage would read: "So this Daniel prospered in the reign of Darius, that is in the reign of Cyrus the Persian." It has also been pointed out that the use of "and" in this sense is not only common in Hebrew, but occurs in the book of Daniel itself. The following instances have been cited: Daniel 1:3 (R.V.), "certain of the children of Israel, *even* of the seed royal." In 6:9, "the document and interdict" becomes "the document" in verse 10, showing they are used as synonymous terms. In 7:1 we read, "he saw a dream, *that is*, visions of his head". Wiseman cites as another example, 1 Chronicles 5:26, which involves the name of a king; and he also points out the harmony of his identification with Isaiah 13:17 and Jeremiah 51:11,28, and also with Ezra 6:2, where the decree of Cyrus is found at Ecbatana.

Wiseman also tells us that in 550 B.C. Media ceased to be a separate nation and became the first satrapy, Mada. From this time on, it was therefore a joint empire, though headed by Cyrus. Nabonidus gives an account of his reign on the Haran stele: in his 10th year (546 B.C.), he refers to "the kings of Egypt, of the Medes, and of the Arabs". Professor Wiseman points out that the king of the Medes at this time, four years after the conquest of Media, can be none other than Cyrus, and concludes that "in Babylon Cyrus used the title 'king of the Medes' in addition to the more usual 'king of Persia'."

Thus unlike Gobryas, "Cyrus is known to have been related to the Medes, to have been called 'king of the Medes' and to have been about sixty years old on becoming king of Babylon". The writer in the *Tyndale Commentary* continues: "While it is true that secular evidence has not yet verified the identification of Darius with Cyrus, there is some corroboration of it in the Greek Bible. In 11:1 the LXX and Theodotion have 'Cyrus' instead of Darius the Mede. This suggests that the Greek translator knew of the double name, and preferred to use the one that was better known to avoid confusing his readers."

The identification of Darius the Mede with Cyrus the Persian, suggested above, appears to harmonise with revelation and history, and to resolve chronological difficulties which arise when years have to be allowed for the reigns of Darius and Cyrus successively. Fuller discussion can be read in *Notes on Some Problems in the Book of Daniel* by D. J. Wiseman (pp. 12-16); and the *Tyndale Commentary* by J. G. Baldwin, pp. 23-28,127.

CHAPTER 6: APPENDIX II

The Lion Symbol

Long before the time of Daniel, lions had been a familiar sight in Palestine and the Euphratean valley, which was the seat of the Assyrian and Babylonian empires. There are quite a number of Old Testament references to them being in Israel; both Samson and David slew lions single-handed. Lions also supplied motifs for gateways to palaces, and to the city of Nineveh. Bas-reliefs in the British Museum portray them being released through gates into a hunting area, where they made 'sport' for the Assyrian bowmen.

The lion is a predatory creature, and therefore is used as a representation of predatory human powers (e.g. Jeremiah 2:14-15; 50:17). The lion is an appropriate symbol at this epoch for the Assyrio-Babylonian beast (Daniel 7:4). Here was a 'den of lions' that attacked Israel. The symbol is also used in another way. In some contexts Israel itself is called a young lion. In Jacob's blessing, Judah is described as a lion; Balaam also has a colourful picture of Israel:

"God brought him forth out of Egypt; he hath as it were the strength of an unicorn: he shall eat up the nations his enemies, and shall break their bones, and pierce them through with his arrows. He couched, he lay down as a lion, and as a great lion: who shall stir him up? Blessed is he that blesseth thee, and cursed is he that curseth thee" (Numbers 24:8-9).

Jesus is the "Lion of the tribe of Judah" (Revelation 5:5), a just predator in this case, a dispenser of judgement and a conqueror.

In some passages attention is drawn to the "roar" of the lion. Such is the loud utterance of the angel of the rainbow (Revelation 10:3), and of the Lord out of Zion (Joel 3:16; Hosea 11:10).

The lion is also used as a figure of the Roman power in the New Testament; it was to the Apostles "an adversary going about as a roaring lion" (1 Peter 5:8).

CHAPTER 7

WE now enter upon the second part of the book. Although still in the section originally written in the Aramaic language, we have passed from the record of the experiences of Babylonian kings and their treatment of the servants of God, to the dream and visions of Daniel himself. It is curious that there is an identity of theme, though not of symbolism, between the first dream of Nebuchadnezzar and the dream of Daniel which happened perhaps as long as 50 years afterwards. Daniel had this dream in the first year of Belshazzar. As we have already seen, Belshazzar was co-regent with his father Nabonidus who reigned 17 years; the *Tyndale Commentary* places the first year of Belshazzar in 552-551 B.C.

As Nebuchadnezzar was granted a preview of the development of the kingdoms of men, until God, by means of "the Stone" which is Christ, destroys them and sets up His own rulership on the earth, so Daniel is shown through the medium of wild beasts the same succession of powers which are finally subjected to judgement, and the kingdom is placed in the hands of the saints. This similarity in the commencement of the two series of revelations gives rise to the possibility of there also being a correspondence between the remaining revelations. This is illustrated on Chart No. 5. The wild beast symbology shows the amoral and sensual character in which the nations of men appear in God's sight—they are like animals.

The First Three Beasts

Daniel would be quite familiar with the appearance of the winged lion, which was the first beast he saw (verses 3-4); every day he would see carved winged beasts like those guarding the palaces at Nineveh and at Babylon. In England we can see examples today which have been excavated and brought to the British Museum. The lion clearly referred to the Assyrian-Babylonian Empire. This had two wings, for sometimes the two states were separate, sometimes joined together. In flight, they wielded supreme power over Asia; but the plumes were cut, and the Babylonian Empire was weakened and divided by the loss of Media and Persia (which countries ultimately overthrew it), but for the time being it remained "erect and rampant".

"A man's heart was given to it." This might seem to be the very opposite of Nebuchadnezzar's symbolic experience, when, during his madness, a beast's heart was given to him. However, he was humbled before God, and with his return to normality he became human again and his throne was restored to him. Some think the symbol means that the character of the Babylonian régime was more humane than the Assyrian had been, which seems indicated by some inscriptions. It could also indicate the point at which Nebuchadnezzar's dream of a man-image develops from the historical situation on which Nebuchadnezzar was meditating when he dreamed. This phase ended with the overthrow of Babylon about 538 B.C..

The second great beast was a bear (verse 5); it had two phases, comprising two dominant kingdoms. It raised itself up on one side, so that the latter phase was the more powerful, but it had only one kind of government, which was despotic. The Median dynasty called Arbacidae merged with the Persians when Cyrus married the daughter of Astyages. In the A.V. the bear is said to have three ribs between its teeth. John Thomas interprets the ribs to relate to the three presidencies referred to in Daniel 6:1-2. The bear was to devour much flesh, which suggests consuming the ribs, and involves the swallowing up of the wealth and revenue of subject provinces. We know that the Persian kings did become phenomenally rich; the feast of Ahasuerus, described in the book of Esther, exemplifies this. This phase lasted until about 330 B.C.

The leopard of verse 6 corresponds with the brazen part of the image. It had four heads and four wings. As with the lion, it is contrary to the decorum of the symbol for this beast to have horns, though its counterpart in chapter 8, the he-goat, has horns. Some treat the heads and wings as meaning practically the same thing; but in the book of Revelation it appears that multiple heads imply successive forms of government, and we suggest it is so here. The Greek beast arose in the West; it was Macedonian. Its stages of development were: 1. Kingship of city-states; 2. A confederacy of these under Philip of Macedon; 3. Alexander's oriental despotism associated with religious adoration, which he introduced having obtained the Persian sovereignty; 4. Following the death of Alexander, a military hierarchy was in control of his empire which continued to be Greek in character.

The leopard had four wings. After Alexander's death his kingdom was divided between his generals. For a time Antigonus tried to

The Babylonian Empire

The Medo-Persian Empire

The Greek Empire

The Roman Empire

63

maintain the unity of the empire, but was killed in 301 B.C. From that time the remaining four generals created the four wings of the imperial area towards the four winds. This divided state lasted from the death of Alexander in 323 B.C. until about 65 B.C., which saw the intrusion of the Romans into the area.

The Fourth Beast

The essence of chapter 7 is in verses 17-18:

"These great beasts, which are four, are four kings, which shall arise out of the earth. But the saints of the most High shall take the kingdom, and possess the kingdom for ever, even for ever and ever".

Daniel then asks for an explanation of the fourth beast which is of such extraordinary appearance. Doubtless he would remember the image and the four metals, and be more interested in the dénouement of the whole affair, than in the details of the intervening stages. Nevertheless details *are* given of the intervening stages, though no interpretation of them is supplied; so it may not be unprofitable to try and fill in the picture. Verse 3 says that the great beasts came up from the sea; but verse 17 tells us that the kings they represented were to arise out of the earth. The "sea" must therefore be a symbolical sea of nations, "whose waters cast up mire and dirt" when strong winds get to work on them.

Daniel betrays great interest in the fourth beast which is so terrifying:

"I would know the truth of the fourth beast, which was diverse from all the others, exceeding dreadful, whose teeth were of iron, and his nails of brass; which devoured, brake in pieces, and stamped the residue with his feet" (verse 19).

This description links the beast with the Roman (iron) aspect of the man-image, through its iron teeth and brass (Greek) nails. We also remember that the two legs of the image foreshadowed the Eastern (Greek) and Western (Latin) aspects of the iron Roman empire. This fourth beast also had "ten horns". Daniel says concerning these:

"I considered the horns, and, behold, there came up among them another little horn, before whom there were three of the first horns plucked up by the roots; and, behold, in this horn were eyes like the eyes of a man, and a mouth speaking great things ... whose look was more stout than its fellows" (verses 18,20).

The interpretation is given us in verses 23-28:

"The ten horns out of this kingdom are ten kings that shall arise: and another shall rise after them; and he shall be diverse from the first, and he shall subdue three kings. And he shall speak great words against the most High, and shall wear out the saints of the most High, and think to change times and laws: and they shall be given into his hand until a time and times and the dividing of time".

When we look back upon 2000 years of Roman supremacy and subsequent division, we realize with hindsight how contracted this description of the development of the fourth beast really is. We know also how that in the New Testament book of Revelation, the telescoped manner of depicting history is more drawn out and expanded, yet even so it is still very compact; but it is not our purpose to go beyond the book of Daniel in this study. The things attributed to the little 11th horn which was in the midst of the ten are so remarkable and so appropriate to the Papacy, that no other application seems possible. The Papal power developed contemporaneously with the invasion of Western Europe by the Gothic nations which set up a group of kingdoms on the Roman territory. There were approximately ten of these, but as they were often contending with one another, the number and identity of them over many years was variable. Many students have compiled lists of the ten horn nations, which vary to some extent according to their conception of the principles of time, character and geography which should in their opinion govern the interpretation. It is true, however, that over a long period, the division of Western Europe into approximately ten kingdoms mainly, if not completely, Gothic in origin, complied with the horn symbolism, and that the Papacy developed contemporaneously with them. These horn kingdoms are the origin of the present nationally divided map of Europe.

The Emperor Constantine started the process by setting up his headquarters at Byzantium, which he then called Constantinople, now known as Istanbul, thus leaving the city of Rome a free field for the Bishop of Rome to acquire more power (see Appendix I). Gothic invasions had commenced even before the time of Constantine, and they continued both during and after his reign. The Patriarch of Rome was also favoured by edicts of subsequent Emperors and began to issue his own ecclesiastical mandates. He was further strengthened by later imperial instruments. "Obedience to the Will of the Roman Bishop was enjoined upon all the churches of the Empire." Such were those of Justinian A.D. 533, and of Phocas, 606/10, who added their authority to Roman supremacy. By degrees the Gothic nations embraced the

Roman faith, at the same time submitting to the Pope's authority. The "little horn", therefore, was different from the rest. It matured later than the others, not as a result of the three who were subdued, for it was in existence already, but because its character was 'different'. It was Papal; at first ecclesiastical but by force of circumstances it was afterwards civil and temporal as well, finally acquiring territory of its very own, as a gift from another horn.

The Scriptural description is remarkably apposite to this power. No other in history matches up with it:

1. It has the "eyes of a man" (verse 8); it claimed a universal episcopate, embracing the spiritual concerns of *all* Christian churches.

2. It had "a mouth speaking great things"; its fulminations even extended to excommunicating kings, putting whole kingdoms under interdicts, and absolving men of their allegiance to their kings or governments.

3. "It spake great words against the most High" (verse 25), accepting titles which were divine prerogatives, such as "Our Lord God the Pope"; "Holy Father", etc.

4. "It changes times and laws", by instituting new articles of faith. It was so contrary to the Law of God, as to develop into "the lawless one" (2 Thessalonians 2:3,8). The Pope claims to be above the law. One of the best known examples of this characteristic was the promulgation of the doctrine of Papal infallibility, concerning which even a zealous Roman Catholic bishop, who was opposed to the intention to proclaim this doctrine said, "If He who reigns above wishes to punish us, making his hand fall heavy on us, as He did on Pharaoh, He has no need to permit Garibaldi's soldiers to drive us away from the eternal city: He has only to let them make Pius IX a god, as we have made a goddess of the blessed virgin. Stop, stop, venerable brethren, on the odious and ridiculous incline on which you have placed yourselves. Save the church from the shipwreck which threatens her, asking from the Holy Scriptures alone for the rule of faith which we ought to believe and to profess. I have spoken; may God help me!"

So spake Bishop Strossmayer in the Vatican Council of 1870, against vehement opposition and cries of "heretic", seeing clearly that to declare the Pope infallible was to *equate him with God*; so that "he as God sitteth in the temple of God, showing himself that he is God" (2 Thessalonians 2:4). Since that time the Roman Church decreed the

Assumption of the Blessed Virgin, in 1950. This doctrine asserts that Mary is in heaven, "not only in soul, but also in body".

5. "It wears out the saints of the most High". This power has in the past exercised a bloodthirsty and persecuting spirit. The doctrine of the infallibility and immutability of the Catholic Church applies in all points which have been authoritatively determined by ecumenical councils. The duty to persecute and exterminate heretics with fire and sword is unreservedly propounded by the third and fourth Lateran Councils.[1] Persecution is therefore inherent in Romanism; it would not appear that this could be repudiated without breaching their principle of infallibility. Today the Catholic Church puts on a more acceptable face, minimising what took place in the past on the score that Protestants persecuted as well: but persecution was only incidental to Protestantism, often because of political involvement by its victims. The stories from history as to what happened to heretics are horrifying to read. The "saints", usually dubbed "heretics", were given into the hands of this power for a definite period of time, specified as "a time, times and a half". The suppression of the Truth in the hands of the "saints" was not to be for ever. The "saints" are not men whose names have been commemorated by a date on the calendar, but are just ordinary believers "called to be saints" (Romans 1:7).

On the principles discussed in the appendix to chapter 4, three-and-a-half times becomes 1260 years (360 day-years to a "time"). From the occasion that the territory of the three horns that fell before the little horn was given over to the Pope, and he became a secular ruler in his own right, as well as a religious ruler, his power increased enormously; but the process of its judgement at the hands of God began at length with the French Revolution in A.D. 1789. The decree of Justinian was in A.D. 533, from which 1260 years brings us to 1793, the date of the "reign of terror" in the middle of the French Revolution. The last ascription of authority to the Pope, as previously noted, was in A.D. 606/10. With 1260 years we are brought to A.D. 1866/70 when the temporal power of the Papacy was broken.

The Papacy still exists, of course, but shorn of its power to persecute. That is why we are able to meet in peace today. It has not always been so. More than 110 years have passed since that time, and the Papacy

---

1. Faber, *The Sacred Calender*, p. 96, cites the third and fourth Lateran Councils. See Concil. Later. III, can. 27, Labb Concil., vol. x, pp. 1522,1523; and Concil. Later. IV, can. 3, Labb. Concil., vol. xi, pp. 147-151

puts on a more "tolerant" face, and professes to work for the reunion of all churches. Really, however, she claims to be their "mistress" and will only be content with their submission, cleverly wrapped up in phraseology though it may be. We must not lose sight of the real character of her blasphemous teachings. "The miracle of the mass" is performed every week by thousands of her priests, but it is "a lying wonder" and we should not cease to look upon it as such, merely because the Papacy lectures the world on morality.

"The judgment shall sit"

The removal of this terrible fourth beast power and its replacement by a world ruled over by "the people of the saints of the most High" (verse 27) is presented in the form of a court of law. It is expressed quite simply in the closing verses of the interpretation. After a reference to the duration of the wearing out of the saints, we read:

"But the judgment shall sit, and they shall take away his dominion, to consume and to destroy it unto the end. And the kingdom and dominion, and the greatness of the kingdom under the whole heaven, shall be given to the people of the saints of the most High, whose kingdom is an everlasting kingdom, and all dominions shall serve and obey him" (verses 26-27).

However, the presentation in the vision Daniel saw is more cryptic (verses 9-14). The prevailing against the saints ceases upon the appearance of one called "the Ancient of days" (verses 21-22,26), and then the judgement is pronounced against the power symbolised by the beast and its horns, because of the great things spoken by the little horn. The judgement was set, and the books were opened:

"I beheld then because of the voice of the great words which the horn spake: I beheld even till the beast was slain, and his body destroyed, and given to the burning flame" (verse 11).

The judgement was according to what was written in the books; and the little horn seems to become identified with the whole beast. Its utterances are given as the reason why the beast is destroyed. It was therefore the controlling influence of the beast.

Thus, with the complete destruction of the fourth beast, there must be complete reorganisation and replacement in Europe; but in verse 12 we are told that the first three beasts lose their dominion, but their lives are prolonged for "a season and a time". Does not this imply that although power passes to Christ and the saints, national entities will continue to exist in the millennium? The prophecy of Isaiah says as much:

> "Egypt . . . shall return even to the Lord, and he shall be intreated of them, and shall heal them . . . In that day shall Israel be the third with Egypt and with Assyria, even a blessing in the midst of the land: whom the Lord of hosts shall bless, saying, Blessed be Egypt my people, and Assyria the work of my hands, and Israel mine inheritance" (19:21-24).

Egypt was part of the Greek empire; that empire with Assyria accounts for the first and third beasts. For the second beast we could refer to Jeremiah:

> "I will set my throne in Elam (i.e. Persia), and will destroy from thence the king and the princes, saith the Lord. But it shall come to pass in the latter days, that I will bring again the captivity of Elam, saith the Lord" (49:38-39).

The Ancient of Days

Who is the "Ancient of days" of verse 9? It has been debated whether he represents the Father Himself, or His manifestation in Christ. The parallel dream of Nebuchadnezzar in Daniel 2 underlines the fact that God rules in the kingdoms of men and giveth them to whomsoever He will. We know from Psalm 2 and other Scriptures that the recipient of the kingdoms is to be the Messiah, Jesus Christ.

Jesus had not yet been born, so he is symbolised by a "stone cut out of the mountain without hands". The emphasis is on the fact that it is *he* who does the destroying of the constituents of the image. Of course, it is God who is "ruling"; and what is done is done not by human might or power, but by His spirit (Zechariah 4:6). In Daniel, this "spirit" is clothed in the symbolic language of manifestation. Instead of a "stone" destroying the image as in chapter 2, we have in chapter 7 "the Ancient of days" judging the fourth beast, and especially its "little horn", for its blasphemous utterances.

> "I beheld then because of the voice of the great words which the horn spake: I beheld even till the beast was slain, and his body destroyed, and given to the burning flame" (verse 11).

The Father has committed all judgement unto the Son: "For as the Father hath life in himself; so hath he given to the Son to have life in himself; and hath given him authority to execute judgement also, because he is the Son of man" (John 5:26-27). Daniel is granted a picture of something that lay long in the future, when Jesus, the Judge, had not yet been born. When he *was* born, this office was accorded to him "because he is the Son of man".

Thus the Judge, sitting as in a court of law, is depicted in symbolic terms, the meaning of which we have to ascertain by comparison with parallel Scriptures. The cryptic description is as follows:

"I beheld till the thrones were cast down, and the Ancient of Days did sit, whose garment was white as snow, and the hair of his head like the pure wool: his throne was like the fiery flame, and his wheels as burning fire. A fiery stream issued and came forth from before him: thousand thousands ministered unto him, and ten thousand times ten thousand stood before him: the judgement was set, and the books were opened" (verses 9,10).

The garments and hair like wool link up with Revelation 1:14, which is obviously a vision relating to Jesus Christ who is depicted *symbolically* as a manifestation of God. The whiteness symbolises righteousness (Revelation 19:8); the throne issuing with a fiery flame infers the destruction of His enemies (cf. Psalm 50:3; 97:3; Isaiah 66:15-16). The wheels as burning fire are connected with the highly symbolic cherubic figures of Ezekiel 10:2-13, which were a similar manifestation to that other contemporary prophet. This cherubic symbolism is in turn derived from the tabernacle of witness symbology, where the cherubim were significantly made "of one piece" with the mercy seat, thus indicating the sameness of nature of redeemer and redeemed. The mercy seat between the cherubim was the place of meeting between God and Moses, on Israel's behalf.

The divine manifestation Daniel saw is called "Ancient of days" because Jesus, when he was granted the Holy Spirit without measure, possessed power which had existed from all eternity. In John's Gospel Jesus speaks from the point of view of this power, which was that of the Father working in him (e.g. John 5:17,19,36; 6:38; 8:18-19, 28-29; 14:10-11). Though Jesus only existed as a person from the time of his birth to Mary, he was manifesting his Father who had existed from all eternity; all he said and did he attributed to his Father—hence the title "Ancient of days".

"The Son of Man"

The judgement of the beast is followed by another judgement introduced by "One like the Son of man".

"I saw in the night visions, and, behold, one like the Son of man came with the clouds of heaven, and came to the Ancient of days, and they brought him near before him. And there was given him dominion, and glory, and a kingdom, that all people, nations, and languages, should serve him: his dominion is an everlasting dominion, which shall not pass away, and his kingdom that which shall not be destroyed" (verses 13-14).

The "One like the Son of man" is a composite body, comprising a multitude of saints who are "conformed to the image of his Son" (Romans 8:29). They receive their reward from the hands of the same Messianic judge. Thus, whereas the fourth beast who wore out the saints is condemned, the "one like the Son of man" is justified, and as a multitudinous Christ receives the same inheritance attributed to "the saints" in verses 22 and 27. The "saints" are all one in Christ Jesus (Galatians 3:28); as Jesus himself prayed, "That they also may be one in us" (John 17:21; see also 1 Corinthians 10:17; Ephesians 2:14-16).

The Effect of the Vision

The effect this vision had on Daniel is described in verses 15 and 28:

"I Daniel was grieved in my spirit in the midst of my body, and the visions of my head troubled me . . . As for me Daniel, my cogitations much troubled me, and my countenance changed in me: but I kept the matter in my heart."

Daniel and ourselves are at opposite ends of the time scale. He must have realised that his spiritual fellows were not only going to suffer persecution, but a persecution which would last for a very long time— and this, too, just at a time when he was anticipating that the release of his people from captivity would be close at hand.

As we shall see later, Daniel was to have several similar shocks, and they upset him emotionally and physically. What should be the effect upon us? Maybe we are no longer persecuted for the doctrines we teach, although we may still be "spoken against", simply because we choose to be different. Has persecution of Christians disappeared for ever? Persecution could easily be resumed if and when war occurs, and if military service becomes even more compelling than it was in previous world wars. There are at least two lessons for us. One is the need to have *faith*; it is abundantly clear that God *has* ruled in the kingdoms of men, and *is still doing so*. Secondly, as saints there is a crown of life laid up for us, that we must on no account allow anyone to take away from us. *We must keep the vision fresh and alive in our hearts.*

Even though the "wearing out" period expired in 1870, yet we still have the contention of the "spirit warring against the flesh"; and we have to experience the light of the Truth against the darkness of the world. The effects of worldly influences are even more insidious without persecution than with it. Therefore:

"We will rejoice in thy salvation, and in the name of our God we will set up our banners; the Lord fulfil all thy petitions ... we are risen, and stand upright. Save, Lord: let the king hear us when we call" (Psalm 20:5-9).

CHAPTER 7: APPENDIX I

Papal Power

In support of the view that the departure of the Emperor from Rome left the Papacy a free field for power development there, Henry T. Hudson, writing in his book *Papal Power* says: "Francesco Guicciardini (1482-1540), in his classic history of the Italian Renaissance, was clearly of this opinion." He claimed that nobody denied "that the transfer of the imperial seat to Constantinople was the first origin of papal power". As a result of the transfer, the Roman pontiffs were left free from Imperial control and they themselves began to assume temporal power. Thomas Hobbes (1588-1679), in his *Leviathan*, described the papacy as "no other than the ghost of the deceased Roman Empire, sitting crowned upon the grave thereof. For so did the papacy start up on a sudden out of the ruins of that heathen power . . . In the time-space continuum of historical happenings, responsibilities of a more secular nature were thrust upon the church . . . In the words of another writer, 'The popes reluctantly took over the role of the Caesars' . . . The transition is not that difficult to understand, for the church was the only institution strong enough to provide necessary leadership" (pp. 16-17).

To begin with, in Apostolic times the Bishop of Rome had nothing to do with politics. But, as we know, apostasy was an ever-present danger, and in A.D. 325 the Emperor Constantine, having overthrown his antichristian rivals, secured the allegiance of the professing Christian party interested in worldly advancement. By this alliance of Church and State spiritual "fornication" was committed. Henry T. Hudson further points out that, by this means, "Christianity became the religion of the empire. The Bishop of Rome had the prestige of association with the imperial metropolis of the world." Both Church and State "were looked upon as being ordained of God and each was granted certain powers within its own respective jurisdiction". Hudson then illustrates how this worked out in practice by quoting a letter written by Pope Gelasius (492-496) to the Emperor Anastasius:

"There are indeed, most august Emperor, two powers by which this world is chiefly ruled: the sacred authority of the popes and royal power. Of these the priestly power is much more important, because it has to render account for the kings of men themselves at the divine tribunal. For you know, our very clement son, that although you have the chief place in dignity over the human race, yet you must submit yourself faithfully to those who have charge of divine things and look to them for the means of your salvation.''

Hudson continues: "In theory, the basis for the later more exorbitant papal claims of authority over the temporal power was therefore present as early as the fifth century" (p. 17).

CHAPTER 8

THE next experience of Daniel is described as a "vision" rather than as a "dream". He sees himself in "Shushan the Palace", which is the city of Susa in the province of Elam, the home city of the Persian emperor. The time is the 3rd year of Belshazzar, which the *Tyndale Commentary* places in 550-549 B.C. Cyrus had established the joint state of the Medes and Persians, and under the veiled hand of God (Isaiah 45:1) he made rapid progress during the next ten years although Babylon had not yet fallen.

"At Shushan in the palace"

We may debate whether Daniel was actually present beside the river Ulai, or simply visualised himself in this place whilst he was actually living in Babylon. One favours the former thought; it was the natural home of the power depicted in this vision by a ram, and Daniel could well have carried out ambassadorial duties there.

The vision was "after that which appeared unto me at the first", which implies that there was a connecting link with the dream of chapter 7. So far, Babylon was the only one of the four kingdoms of men identified by name; that was as the head of gold of the image of chapter 2. In the present vision, Daniel sees a two-horned ram, which the chapter itself identifies with the Medo-Persian power (verse 20), with its characteristic higher phase arising later.

The ram pushed westward, northward, and southwards. No doubt Daniel knew that the aggressive ram had already been attacking Greece in its westward expeditions, before Cyrus had ever moved against Babylon. God revealed to Daniel how the Persian successors of Cyrus were going to be superseded by a Greek "goat" leader. The conflict is very graphically described. The goat is so stirred up that his feet hardly touch the ground, so great is the animosity and speed with which he propels himself along in his desire to attack the ram (verses 6-8). So the ram and the goat fill in the picture of the silver and brass, or the bear and the leopard of the previous visions, informing us that they represent Medo-Persia and Greece respectively.

75

THE PROPHECY OF DANIEL

Though the angelic description and interpretation of the vision leaves us in no doubt about who the ram and goat represent, it passes over them rather lightly, and concentrates more upon the development of the four horns, which grow up in place of the first great horn of the goat after it is broken. These, and the "little horn" which grows out of one of the four, are not identified, but left to our interpretation according to history. The more remote the future, the less detailed the symbolism.

We tend to describe this chapter as the vision of the ram and the he-goat, but the object of the vision is to reveal the "last end of the indignation" (verse 19)—the reason for the length of time occupied in "the treading down of the sanctuary" (verse 13). Consequently the *angelic* description is "the vision concerning the daily sacrifice" (verse 13), or "the vision of the evening and the morning" (verse 26). This fact also brings to us the realisation that with chapter 8 we are back in the Hebrew language section of the book, and therefore the land of Israel and the Jewish people form the centre and core of the revelation.

Although there were still some years to go, we can assume that Daniel had been anticipating the restoration of his fellow-Jews to their homeland in fulfilment of Jeremiah's prophecies, when the beast-dream shattered his equanimity with the information that a long period of persecution lay in store for the people of God. What, then, is to be said of the effect upon him two years later, of this fresh news that despite a regathering, he sees displayed before him the destruction of everything the faithful Jew held dear, even to the destruction of his Messianic Prince? Not only so, but the time scale is so long: it is horrifying—he dared not contemplate it. Daniel was appalled and ill for days (verse 27).

One "as the appearance of a man" approached Daniel and was addressed as Gabriel by "a man's voice between the banks of Ulai" (verses 15,16). This "voice" is not identified in the vision, but the circumstances are similar to chapter 10, where "a certain man" speaking from between the banks of the river is described in great detail (10:4,5). The river is different, but the comparison is strong enough to suggest that we have here a hint of the principle we shall have to deal with when we come to the later chapter.

Be that as it may, the angel Gabriel is called upon to explain. He says, "Understand, O son of man" (see Appendix II on this messianic title). At his approach Daniel was afraid, and fell upon his face, undergoing a symbolic death and resurrection, showing that "the time of the end"

The Ram

The He-Goat

will be fulfilled in that event. "For at the time appointed the end shall be" (verse 19). So Gabriel promises to make Daniel to know "what shall be in the *last end of the indignation*" (verses 16-19), and he proceeds to explain in verses 20-23, but we will leave consideration of "the king of fierce countenance" for the present.

Gabriel's remarks take us back to verse 8 and to the breaking of the great Greek horn of Alexander, as a result of which four notable horns emerge. The prophecy continues:

"And out of one of them came forth a little horn, which waxed exceeding great, toward the south, and toward the east, and toward the pleasant land. And it waxed great, even to the host of heaven; and it cast down some of the host and of the stars to the ground, and stamped upon them. Yea, he magnified himself even to (margin: against) the prince of the host, and by him the daily sacrifice was taken away, and the place of his sanctuary was cast down. And an host was given him against the daily sacrifice by reason of transgression, and it cast down the truth to the ground: and it practised, and prospered" (verses 9-12).

77

Then the question is put:

"How long shall be the vision concerning the daily sacrifice, and the transgression of desolation, to give both the sanctuary and the host to be trodden under foot? And he said unto me, Unto two thousand and three hundred days (margin: evening mornings); then shall the sanctuary be cleansed (margin: justified)" (verses 13,14).

After the incident of Daniel's symbolic death and resurrection, Gabriel comments upon the breaking of the great Greek horn, and then continues in verse 22:

"Now that being broken, whereas four stood up for it, four kingdoms shall stand up out of the nation, but not in his power. And in the latter time of their kingdom, when the transgressors are come to the full, a king of fierce countenance, and understanding dark sentences, shall stand up. And his power shall be mighty, but not by his own power: and he shall destroy wonderfully, and shall prosper, and practise, and shall destroy the mighty and the holy people. And through his policy also he shall cause craft to prosper in his hand; and he shall magnify himself in his heart, and by peace shall destroy many: he shall also stand up against the Prince of princes; but he shall be broken without hand. And the vision of the evening and the morning which was told is true: wherefore shut thou up the vision; for it shall be for many days" (verses 22-26).

This short but cryptic pronouncement surveys a vast vista of the purpose of God, spread over long ages. The arena is "the pleasant land"—God's land, Israel (Jeremiah 3:19; Ezekiel 20:6,15; Psalm 48:2; Zechariah 7:14). "The host of heaven" and "the stars" are the priests and officials of Israel. The same sort of language is used in Isaiah 14:13-14, when Isaiah envisaged the king of Babylon as the morning star, Lucifer, the ambitious aspirant to the throne in Jerusalem. The "host" or army of God, are the Jewish people.

With hindsight we can detect both the bitter and the sweet aspects of the mission that had to be carried through "*by reason of transgression*". "All have sinned and come short of the glory of God". John the Baptist directs attention to "the Lamb of God that taketh away the sin of the world". The evening-morning sacrifices of lambs were a daily offering instituted at Mount Sinai to teach this lesson (Exodus 29:38-42); yet they never could, by themselves, accomplish the desired removal of sin. The law "was added *because of transgressions*, till the seed should come to whom the promise was made" (Galatians 3:19).

"So the law was put in charge to lead us to Christ that we might be justified by faith" (verse 24, N.I.V.). Thus was "the precious blood of Christ (shed), as of a lamb without blemish and without spot: who verily was foreordained before the foundation of the world, but was manifest in these last times" (1 Peter 1:19).

The Jewish priests offered "oftentimes the same sacrifices, which can never take away sins: but this man, after he had offered one sacrifice for sins for ever, sat down on the right hand of God; from henceforth expecting till his enemies be made his footstool. For by one offering he hath perfected for ever them that are sanctified" (Hebrews 10:11-14). For this removal of sin and the consequent life to be achieved, the seed of the woman had to be bruised in the heel (Genesis 3:15): Jesus had to die. *This is what this vision is all about*, and it is amplified in chapter 9.

In verse 12, a "host" not of Israel, is permitted by God to work its will against what is holy "by reason of transgression" as a punishment for the sins of God's people. Some interpret the words as meaning "with transgression", that is by Gentiles introducing what is an "abomination" to God. The further reference to "when the transgressors are come to the full" (verse 23) is also understood by some to mean the wicked ones of Israel; yet others read, with the Greek, "transgression", and apply the words to the Gentiles.

It seems more appropriate to apply the "transgression" abstractly to both, and the "little horn" (or "the king of fierce countenance") perpetrating, in conjunction with the Jews, the last word in sinfulness by encompassing the death of God's own Son.

> " 'Twas on that dark and mournful night
> When Jews and Gentiles joined their power
> Against the Son of God to fight,
> To mock his name, his life devour."

And so they prevailed against "The Prince of the Host". ("Prince"— in the Hebrew *Sar;* cf. Isaiah 9:6, "The Prince of Peace".)

After some years the death of the Prince was followed by the removal of the Mosaic ritual, the place where it was performed, and the treading underfoot of its devotees. This resulted in the total eclipse and dispersion of the whole nation for a very long time. No wonder God was indignant; this experience of the Jews is the expression of His indignation.

"The indignation" is a word used of God's anger against Israel in other passages (e.g. Isaiah 10:5; Ezekiel 22:24,31); but perhaps more frequently of all the Gentile nations (e.g. Isaiah 26:20; 30:27; Jeremiah 50:25; Nahum 1:6; Habakkuk 3:12). Zephaniah 3:8 is a good illustration:

"Therefore wait ye upon me, saith the Lord, until the day that I rise up to the prey: for my determination is to gather the nations, that I may assemble the kingdoms, to pour upon them mine *indignation*, even all my fierce anger: for all the earth shall be devoured with the fire of my jealousy."

Jews and Gentiles are both implicated in wickedness against God, and the "last end of the indignation" surely indicates the limit God has placed upon the display of His anger, when it gives place to mercy and joy in the Kingdom of God.

Should we not reflect on the fact that *all men* are the creation of God's hand, and yet how little recognition of the fact they render back to Him? On the contrary, judged on the principle that "actions speak louder than words" there is almost universal rejection of any acknowledgement of His existence, or of any responsibility to Him. How true are the words of Job: "They spend their days in wealth, and in a moment go down to the grave. Therefore they say unto God, Depart from us; for we desire not the knowledge of thy ways. What is the Almighty that we should serve him? And what profit should we have, if we pray unto him?" (21:13-15).

As associates of Jesus, shall we not take note of the situation, and plead with the Psalmist in the beautiful refrain in Psalm 107: "Oh that men would praise the Lord for his goodness, and for his wonderful works to the children of men" (verse 15). "Whoso is wise, and will observe these things, even they shall understand the lovingkindness of the Lord?" (verse 43). And respond again with the Psalmist, "What shall I render unto the Lord for all his benefits toward me?" (116:12).

How long the Down-treading?

Whilst the Babylonian supremacy was still operative, the revelations of this eighth chapter conveyed to Daniel events which would develop in the near future, but gradually receding into the very remote future; not as before, by a detailed description of successive kingdoms of men, but by the recurring downtreading of Jewry after the forthcoming restoration of Daniel's people to their own land. The question "How long?" is answered by "Unto 2300 evening-mornings" (verses 13,14), during which period sacrifices would fail to be offered, and the oppressing "king" would himself ultimately be destroyed by the divine hand of the Prince of Princes.

From Daniel's standpoint the *end* was so distant, that beyond the first few years the detail given is vague, and would not be understood until the events themselves revealed the meaning. This also applies to the period itself which is deliberately obscure. The 2300 evening-mornings, if interpreted as that number of years, cannot apply to the earliest events seen in the vision, because they have already been overtaken by the passage of time, and still the Prince of Princes has not intervened. The point of action when the ram's horn was broken by Alexander is already over 2300 years ago, as is also the breaking of the Goat's great horn in the death of Alexander himself. The battle of Ipsus in A.D. 301 saw the emergence of *four horns*, which is a very relevant detail and has an end-point not very far into the future from the time of writing. It is a little obscure whether the 2300 applies to one of the stages in the political developments of the vision, or to the actual suspension of the evening-morning sacrifice, which can be equated with downtreading of Jewry, and the existence of the abomination of desolation. In the A.V., verse 13 reads, "How long shall be the vision concerning the daily sacrifice, and the transgression of desolation (margin: making desolate), to give both the sanctuary and the host to be trodden under-foot?" The threatened judgements of Leviticus 26:27-33 were being recalled as early as the days of Ahaz, in Micah 6:13: "Therefore I have begun to smite you, making you desolate because of your sins" (R.S.V.).

What appears to be certain is:

1. That the "little horn" equates with "the king of fierce countenance".

2. That he is to be destroyed by the Prince of Princes by divine power; therefore he is still in existence.

3. That the down-treading lasts for 2300 evening-mornings, a time-period which is not yet exhausted—clearly the "continual burnt offering" is not now being offered.

4. That the sacrifices were suspended by Antiochus Epiphanes between 168 and 165 B.C., and by Titus in A.D. 70, or rendered obsolete by the collaboration of Herod, Pilate and the High Priests ca. A.D. 30.

Whilst the offering of the evening and morning lambs was suppressed, they were to remain "without a king, without a prince, and without a sacrifice" for "many days" (Hosea 3:4). The cleansing of the anti-typical Holy of Holies is already past, as we shall see in considering chapter 9. In fact the "little horn" was instrumental in bringing that about. Doubtless it is the literal sanctuary that is in question.

In the end the Prince of Princes destroys the persistent enemy "without hand" (verse 25). Then shall the holy be avenged. In the meantime, "Judah's host for its rebellion against Yahweh was to become an evening-morning sacrifice until the end of a period of 2300 years."[1] The king of fierce countenance, whose emergence seems to coincide with the "little horn", is described in four short verses, yet covers a period practically synonymous in length with the 2300 evening-mornings. Can it be that this king-figure is a personification of the *sin* with which the Prince of the Host has so valiantly contended— rather than representing an individual ruler to be identified in history? He is a condensed picture of all the anti-God rulers from Antiochus Epiphanes through pagan and Papal Rome, Turk, and whatever manifestation may take command in the days that lie ahead until Messiah comes in power.

The "little horn", alias "the king of fierce countenance", after treading down the truth, continues to practise and to prosper until the end of the 2300 evening-mornings. It sees its ultimate encounter with the glorified Prince of Princes when the tables are turned, and now the king "shall be broken without hand". This final destiny merges into the work of the "stone which was cut from the mountain without hands", and performed the will of God, by subjugating the nations of the world (Daniel 2:34,45).

The phrase "without hands" means without human hands and is a Bible idiom for "with divine hands", that is, by Divine intervention. It is synonymous with "Not by might, nor by power, but by my spirit, saith the Lord of Hosts" (Zechariah 4:6).[2]

---

1. J. Thomas, *Exposition of Daniel*, p. 28; later the author adopted the reading 2400 instead of 2300.
2. See Appendix III

CHAPTER 8: APPENDIX I

The Ram and the He-Goat and their Days

In the vision an aggressive ram with two horns is said to represent the kings of Media and Persia (verses 3-4,20). The ram is opposed by the he-goat, which slays the ram with its one great horn. This very aptly represents Alexander the Great, who overthrew the Persian overlordship, and took Babylon under his wing, thus becoming identifiable with the brazen part of the Image.

His reign was short-lived; his death in 323 B.C., leaving an heir as yet unborn, also left the field open for his generals to divide the empire between them. To begin with there were five of them. Antigonus, an old man, who was committed to the principle of *unification*, and who held Anatolia and Syria, was eliminated at the battle of Ipsus in 301 B.C. This left four generals represented by the horns, but their internecine strife gradually reduced the remaining effective powers to two, the Seleucids becoming consolidated in Syria and northern and eastern provinces, and the Ptolemies in the south in Egypt. The "successor states had assumed their definitive form" circa 280 B.C.[1]

Israel, lying between these two contestants, suffered from their rivalries, the Persian protection now having been lost. This was particularly the case from around 200 B.C.

Sicily and the south coast of Italy had been part of the sphere of influence of Alexander. The Romans overcame the Italian states to the the north, and were eventually able to confront Carthage. After discussing Rome's war with Carthage, Colin McEvedy says, "No sooner was the long struggle over than Rome had to turn east where, after the death of Ptolemy IV (203) Egypt had fallen into disarray that excited Seleucid and Macedonian appetites".[1]

Thus commenced the Roman intrusion into the arena of the prophecy. In 197 B.C. the Romans had beaten Philip V of Macedon, and required the respect of that country. In 190 B.C. they routed Antiochus near Magnesia and in 171-168 again attacked Macedon which they annexed in 148. In coming to the aid of Egypt, they contributed (maybe quite

---

1. Colin McEvedy, *The Penguin Atlas of Ancient History*, pp. 62,68

unintentionally) to the affliction of the Jews. Commenting upon this Roman intrusion, William Fairweather writes: "In 168 B.C., Antiochus (Epiphanes) set out on his last Egyptian campaign. Just as he was ready to grasp his prize, and stood once more within sight of Alexandria, Popilius Laenas, the ambassador of the Imperial Senate, suddenly appeared, and charged him to abandon all hostile measures against Egypt if he valued the friendship of the Romans. Antiochus evasively said he would consider the matter. But the proud Roman, drawing a circle round him with his staff, ordered him to make his decision before he moved from the spot. Brought thus to bay, Antiochus prudently promised to respect the Roman demand. Thwarted in his schemes against Egypt, the tyrant determined to stamp out once for all the Jewish religion in Palestine".[2] Thus were precipitated the dreadful experiences of the Jews of 168-167 B.C. The desecration of the Temple which followed appears to have lasted for precisely three years. After its rededication, the sacrificial offerings do not appear to have been interrupted until the time of Titus in A.D. 70, except in the sense that they were rendered obsolete by the crucifixion, about A.D. 30.

It could still be argued that since the intervention of Antiochus Epiphanes, even the rededication was not completely according to the law, because the High-priesthood had become a political appointment agreed with the Seleucids, and later with the Roman overlords. The office ceased to be occupied by men of Aaronic descent, but was obtained by intrigue, bribery, and by unforgiveable concessions to Hellenism by ambitious Jews.

To revert to the period of Roman intrusion, they followed up the annexation of Macedonia in 148 B.C., with that of Achaia in 146, Asia in 133, Cyrene in 74, Syria in 66, Jerusalem in 63 (under Pompey), and Egypt in 31. Thus the Romans began to get involved just after the time of Ptolemy IV, ca. 200 B.C., and ended with the complete overthrow of Jerusalem and the destruction of the Temple by Titus, due to Jewish revolt, in A.D. 70.

As to the question of "how long" the down-treading of the sanctuary was to continue, we are told, "Unto two thousand and three hundred days (evening-mornings)".[3] Which overthrow and downtreading was

2. Wm. Fairweather, *From the Exile to the Advent*, p. 127
3. H. Grattan Guinness, *The Approaching End of the Age*, p. 402. Summarises the work of M. de Cheseaux, in reference to prophetic periods having an astronomical basis. His work was published in 1754. It does not seem possible for this to have been known to the astronomers of Daniel's day.

envisaged? There seem to be only two possibilities: first, that by Antiochus Epiphanes in 167 B.C., which precipitated the Maccabaean uprising; in this case, the desecration of the Temple lasted three years precisely according to 1 Maccabees 1:54; 4:52. Second, that by Titus in A.D. 70, when the overthrow was permanent.

Are the 2300 evening-mornings literal days, or do they represent a long period? Antiochus Epiphanes reigned 11 years in all, part of the time as co-regent with an infant heir. The infant was assassinated in his absence, leaving him sole ruler from 170 to 164 B.C, that is 6 years. 2300 literal days equal 6 years and about 4½ months, so a literal application cannot be fitted in very well. On the other hand we have the statements, "At the time of the end shall be the vision" (verse 17); "the last end of the indignation: for at the time appointed the end shall be" (verse 19), associated with the symbolic death and resurrection of Daniel himself, all indicating that a long period is envisaged.

When Cyrus restored the Jews to Judea where they established a protected province, a new Temple was built by Zerubbabel between 520 and 516 B.C., which lasted about 500 years. It was rebuilt by king Herod in 46 years from 16 B.C. to A.D. 30. Accepting that a long period is involved, and that the basis for computation is the day-for-a-year principle previously discussed, how should we apply the dating? If we felt compelled to count 2300 years from the desecration of the Temple by Antiochus Epiphanes in 167 B.C., we should feel as "astonished" as Daniel did when the vision was granted to him, for it takes us to A.D. 2133; how much more if we counted from Titus' overthrow in A.D. 70! In considering the "seven times" of Daniel 4, one possibility is to calculate from the cutting down of the tree, that is from the fall of Babylon; not from the first event seen in the vision, but from *the point of action* taken by the Persians cutting the tree down.

Applying this principle to chapter 8, we find two or three points of action. The first is the breaking of the Persian ram's horns and stamping on its body; a second point is the breaking of the Greek goat's horn—the death of Alexander. In the first alternative, Alexander's Persian campaign, 2300 years span from 332-330 B.C. to A.D. 1969-71. In the second case, from 323 B.C. to A.D. 1978. There is also a third possibility. In his interpretation, the angel Gabriel makes pointed allusion to the emergence of *four horns*. This did not happen immediately after the death of Alexander, by reason of the activities of Antigonus referred to earlier. He delayed the open emergence of four horns until the battle of Ipsus in 301 B.C.; 2300 years from which time brings us to A.D. 2000.

The first suggested ending is not without significance, for it closely approximates to the re-unification of Jerusalem in 1967. The second was characterised by the making of peace with Egypt and the invasion by Israel of South Lebanon, and who knows to what that may lead? It may also be that such periods are to be understood as "characteristic" of the age, and to have more than one application from stages in the process at the beginning, to stages in the ending of the scope of the vision. When the sanctuary is "cleansed", "justified" or "avenged", Gentile down-treading will be a thing of the past and the Land freed.

CHAPTER 8: APPENDIX II

The Son of Man

The Messianic title "Son of man" accorded to the contemporary prophet Ezekiel throughout his book (e.g. 2:1,3 etc.), is accorded to Daniel but once directly (8:17): "Understand, O son of man: for at the time of the end shall be the vision". In chapter 10 there are two less direct allusions which nevertheless fit in with the MAN theme of the prophecy: "O Daniel, a *man* greatly beloved, *understand* the words that I speak unto thee" (verse 11); "O *man* greatly beloved, fear not: peace be unto thee, be strong, yea, be strong" (verse 19).

The title is appropriated by Jesus in the context of his reference to Daniel's prophecy of "the abomination that maketh desolate", with the same contextual reference to *understanding*: "Whoso readeth, let him understand" (Matthew 24:15; Daniel 9:27; 11:31; 12:11). The impending judgements Jesus foretells in his Mount Olivet discourse are associated with the "coming of the Son of man" (Matthew 24:27): "And then shall appear the sign of the Son of man in heaven: and then shall all the tribes of the earth mourn, and they shall see the Son of man coming in the clouds of heaven with power and great glory" (verse 30). Again, before Caiaphas, Jesus confesses, "Hereafter shall ye see the Son of man sitting on the right hand of power, and coming in the clouds of heaven" (26:64). "Coming in the clouds of heaven" is a further allusion to Daniel 7:13, and the symbolic multitudinous body of Christ redeemed and justified.

Jesus links the title with Daniel again, when he connects himself with the judge at the resurrection, quoting Daniel 12:2 in John 5:25-27:

> "The hour is coming, and now is, when the dead shall hear the voice of the Son of God: and they that hear shall live. For as the Father hath life in himself; so hath he given to the Son to have life in himself; and hath given him authority to execute judgement also, because he is the Son of man".

Both expressions, "Son of God" and "Son of man" involve the virgin birth by Mary as a fundamental tenet of the Gospel. Although the formula is Son of *man*, the Fatherhood of God necessitates the understanding of this expression to be son of *woman*—Divine begettal through a mortal human female. Hence the expressions, "seed of the woman" (Genesis 3:15), "the handmaid of the Lord" (Psalm 86:16; Luke 1:38).

Jesus *was* son of man, the son of a "handmaid"; he bore the divine delineation of character for the "declaration of the righteousness of God", and he bore human nature for "the condemnation of sin, in the flesh". He repeatedly used the title "Son of man". Even when facing the accusing High Priest and acknowledging his claim to be the Son of God, he presents this other side of his Messiahship.

CHAPTER 8: APPENDIX III

"Broken without hand"

Other comparable illustrations of the idiom are as follows:

Acts 7:48; 17:24-25; 19:26—

God "dwelleth not in temples made with hands". "They be no gods, which are made with hands."

2 Corinthians 5:1; Hebrews 9:11,24—

"We have a house ... not made with hands". Christ is become a high priest by a "more perfect tabernacle, not made with hands ... not of this building".

Ephesians 2:11—

"Circumcision in the flesh made by hands". Contrast Colossians 2:11—"Circumcision made without hands, in putting off the body of sin".

Job 34:20 (cf. verses 12-15)—

If the spirit of God is withdrawn, "In a moment shall they die ... taken away without hand."

Lamentations 4:6—

Like Sodom, "overthrown as in a moment ... no hands stayed on her."

CHAPTER 9

ABOUT 13 years have slipped by since Daniel saw the vision of chapter 8. The overthrow of the Babylonian dynasty resulting in the accession of Darius the Mede (alias Cyrus the Persian?—see page 57), naturally turned Daniel's thoughts to the effect it would have on the Jewish community. He realised the 70 years captivity spoken of by Jeremiah was on the point of expiry, and he set himself by prayer and supplication to seek the face of God.

Daniel's Prayer

What Jeremiah had said is recorded in chapter 25 of his prophecy. He had been reproving the inhabitants of Judah and Jerusalem in God's name since the 13th year of king Josiah. In the 23rd year he proceeded to say that because they would not hearken, the whole land would be given into the hand of Nebuchadrezzar king of Babylon, and Judah and the surrounding countries would be desolated:

"This whole land shall be a desolation, and an astonishment; and these nations shall serve the king of Babylon seventy years" (verse 11).

After that, it would be Babylon's turn:

"And it shall come to pass, when seventy years are accomplished, that I will punish the king of Babylon, and that nation, saith the Lord, for their iniquity, and the land of the Chaldeans, and will make it perpetual desolations" (verse 12).

There was, however, a comforting reassurance in the words of Jeremiah in a later chapter:

"For thus saith the Lord, That after seventy years be accomplished at Babylon I will visit you, and perform my good word towards you, in causing you to return to this place" (29:10).

The history of how all this came to pass after the death of king Josiah may be read in 2 Chronicles chapter 36.

In common with other prophets, although personally a righteous man, Daniel associates himself with the faithless people, and pleads

90

with God on their behalf, confessing their sins. He does so to a God who is great and dreadful, "keeping covenant and mercy to them that love him".

"We have sinned, and have committed iniquity, and have done wickedly, and have rebelled, even by departing from thy precepts and from thy judgements ... O Lord, righteousness belongeth unto thee, but unto us confusion of faces, as at this day ... unto all Israel, that are near, and that are far off, through all the countries whither thou hast driven them, because of their trespass that they have trespassed against thee ... O Lord, according to all thy righteousness, I beseech thee, let thine anger and thy fury be turned away from thy city Jerusalem, thy holy mountain: because for our sins, and for the iniquities of our fathers, Jerusalem and thy people are become a reproach to all that are about us ... Hear the prayer of thy servant ... cause thy face to shine upon thy sanctuary that is desolate, for the Lord's sake ..." (9:5,7,16-17).

Daniel concludes with an abrupt, emphatic and urgent appeal:

"O Lord, hear; O Lord, forgive; O Lord, hearken and do; defer not, for thine own sake, O my God: for thy city and thy people are called by thy name" (verse 19).

Such is the heart-rending pleading. Because God had delivered Israel from Egypt (Jeremiah 32:20), He might be persuaded to repeat the deliverance by restoring His sanctuary at Jerusalem—*for His own sake*. God had chosen Jerusalem to cause His *Name* to dwell there (Deuteronomy 12:11). He Himself had deigned to dwell there (Psalm 9:11). The same point is made in Ezra 6:12, where Darius uses the words, "God hath caused his name to dwell there," and by Nehemiah, who in his prayer, refers to God regathering Israel "unto the place that I have chosen to set (or tabernacle) my name there" (1:9).

The words of Daniel's prayer remind us of the manifestation vouchsafed to Moses when, in the cleft of the rock:

"The Lord passed by before him, and proclaimed, The LORD, the LORD God, merciful and gracious, longsuffering, and abundant in goodness and truth, keeping mercy for thousands, forgiving iniquity and transgression and sin, and that will by no means clear the guilty; visiting the iniquity of the fathers upon the children, and upon the children's children, unto the third and to the fourth generation" (Exodus 34:6-7).

The terms "iniquity, transgression and sin" are echoed in Daniel's prayer. Each term has its own particular meaning, though they are sometimes used in parallel. All are opposed to the righteousness of God.

God's answer to this prayer comes immediately in the form of a visit from Gabriel, the angel who had been his interpreter in the previous vision (8:15), and who, long years after Daniel had passed away, was to be intimately concerned in matters to do with the coming of the Messiah (Luke 1:19,26). Another connecting link with the earlier vision is that Gabriel touched Daniel "about the time of the evening oblation (3 p.m.)" (verse 21). It had been the vision concerning the "daily" or "evening-morning" sacrifice, the "continual burnt offering", which pointed to the antitypical sacrifice of Jesus, perhaps but dimly perceived in Old Testament times.

Whereas chapter 8 deals with the long time that was to elapse before the sanctuary and the land will be delivered from the downtreading of abominations which so distressed Daniel, chapter 9 is more comforting and more specific in defining the shorter time when the Messiah himself should come; and though he would suffer at the hands of those who should have supported him, he would by that means make possible the ultimate redemption.

The "commandment" is the *Word* (margin), the message of verses 24-27. Daniel was "greatly beloved"; through him God was pleased to make known His purpose for the benefit of other loved ones who might be privileged to understand. Let us therefore try to understand the Word and consider the Vision.

The Prophecy of the Seventy Weeks

Gabriel says:

> "Seventy weeks are determined (decreed) upon thy people and upon thy holy city, to finish the transgression, and to make an end of sins, and to make reconciliation for iniquity, and to bring in everlasting righteousness, and to seal up the vision and prophecy, and to anoint the most Holy" (verse 24).

This statement is parallelled by a passage extending the period from a decree to restore and to build Jerusalem, to the cutting off of Messiah the Prince (verses 24-26). The culmination of the prophecy is expressed in six clauses: three aspects of sin (the same as those spoken of to Moses), and three of righteousness.

1. "Transgression" (Heb. *pasha*) is defined as rebellion against lawful authority, and thus constitutes presumptuous sin. To this, the word "finish" is prefixed, indicating the idea to shut, restrain, or close it.

2. "Sin" (Heb. *chatah*), to stumble; shortcoming, not necessarily wilful, but blameworthy. "To make an end" of this, is to finish or seal up the wickedness.

3. "Iniquity" (Heb. *avah*) is defined as perverseness, wrong. To "make reconciliation" in regard to this, is to cover, or make atonement for it.

The ultimate transgression against God would be committed in the slaying of His own Son, and which in itself God would turn into the provision of an Atonement. Daniel's intercession brought God's answering mercy: "iniquity, transgression and sin" were to be completely done away in all their forms. "Behold the Lamb of God, which taketh away the sin of the world" says John the Baptist (John 1:29); it is "sin" in the abstract as Daniel envisages it. Animal sacrifices indeed gained forgiveness for individual sins (Leviticus 4:20,26 etc.), but man sinned again, and a further sacrifice became necessary; and in the end he still died. These offerings "could not make the comers thereunto perfect" (Hebrews 9:9; 10:1,11); therefore God's righteousness is to remove the *consequences* of sin as well as to cover the faults and errors. So a threefold complement is added:

"to bring in everlasting righteousness";

"to seal up the vision and prophecy";

"to anoint a Holy of holies".

1. *"To bring in everlasting righteousness"*: The "righteousness" of the first clause was the burden of other prophets also. For example: "I bring near my righteousness; it shall not be far off, and my salvation shall not tarry: and I will place salvation in Zion for Israel my glory" (Isaiah 46:13). "He saw that there was no man, and wondered that there was no intercessor; therefore his arm brought salvation unto him; and his righteousness, it sustained him. For he put on righteousness as a breastplate, and an helmet of salvation upon his head; and put on the garments of vengeance for clothing, and was clad with zeal as a cloke" (Isaiah 59:16, etc.). Jesus was "brought in" as the first-begotten, and it was said, "Let all the angels of God worship him" (Hebrews 1:6). Within the decreed period Jesus was slain and raised again to the divine nature, to become "our righteousness" and that we might become

"the righteousness of God in him" (1 Corinthians 1:30; 2 Corinthians 5:21). By this means *death*, the consequence of sin, was to be abolished.

2. *"To seal up the vision and prophecy"*: "Seal up" is the same term as "make an end of", as applied to "sins" in the same verse. It was completed. Of himself Jesus said, "him hath God the Father sealed" (John 6:27). Peter says, "Those things which God before had shewed by the mouth of all his prophets, that Christ should suffer, he hath so fulfilled" (Acts 3:18). The vision was sealed in that all that had been prophesied was fulfilled, or finished, and God's righteousness was vindicated.

3. *"To anoint the most Holy"*: This is the A.V. rendering. Pusey tells us that the article here is indefinite: "The remaining clause, 'and to anoint an All-holy', must be spiritual, since all else is spiritual." He goes on to explain, " 'Holy of holies', lit. 'holiness of holinesses', that is All-holiness, is a ritual term, used to express the exceeding holiness which things acquire by being consecrated to God. It is never used to describe a place, but is always an attribute of the thing, and, in one place, of the person, who is spoken of. *It is most holy! Aaron was separated, to hallow him all-holy.*[1] The destruction of the temple, as having been previously profaned, is the close of this prophecy. The prophecy promised *an All-holy*, which should be anointed, for *the holy place* which should be destroyed; as our Lord speaks of 'the temple of his body'."

After discussing the title "Holy One", and "the Anointing", Pusey goes on, "This symbolical meaning of the anointing is fixed by the next words of the prophecy: 'unto Messiah the Prince'. The word is repeated. The last of the six blessings was, 'to anoint an All-holy': *limshoach kodesh kodashim*. He resumes at once, 'unto one Anointed, a Prince': *ad Mashiach nagid*. No-one, wishing to be understood, would unite so closely words, relating to the same period of time, the end of the 70 weeks, had they not related to the same object: '*to anoint* an All-holy'; 'unto one *Anointed*'. The words probably fixed the use of the name *Messiah* or *the Messiah*, *Christ*, or *the Christ*, as that of the long-expected Redeemer".[2]

1. 1 Chronicles 23:13; see R.V.m. and also Berkeley version
2. E. B. Pusey, *Daniel the Prophet: Nine Lectures*, pp. 181-183, 3rd ed., 1869 (author's italics)

We now address ourselves to the time-period of 70 weeks mentioned in verse 24, and trace its unfolding in verses 25-27, which read as follows:

"Know therefore and understand, that from the going forth of the commandment to restore and to build Jerusalem unto the Messiah the Prince shall be seven weeks, and threescore and two weeks: the street shall be built again, and the wall, even in troublous times. And after threescore and two weeks shall Messiah be cut off, but not for himself: and the people of the prince that shall come shall destroy the city and the sanctuary; and the end thereof shall be with a flood, and unto the end of the war desolations are determined. And he shall confirm the covenant with many for one week: and in the midst of the week he shall cause the sacrifice and the oblation to cease, and for the overspreading of abominations he shall make it desolate, even until the consummation, and that determined shall be poured upon the desolator."

The period is divided up into three parts: 7 weeks, 62 weeks, and 1 week divided in the midst. This means 49 years, 434 years, and 7 years divided in half, or 486½ plus 3½ years.

As in the overthrow of the Jewish state and the fall of Jerusalem there were several stages, so there were also several stages in its restoration; consequently there were several points which were 70 years apart, or approximately so, during the captivities and the return which can be traced on the chronological chart. Thus "the going forth of the commandment" was issued in four stages. But first let us look at the prophecy about Cyrus uttered by Isaiah about 100 years before the prophecy of Jeremiah:

"That saith of Cyrus, He is my shepherd, and shall perform all my pleasure: even saying to *Jerusalem*, Thou shalt be built; and to the temple, Thy foundation shall be laid. Thus saith the Lord to his anointed, to Cyrus ... I have raised him up in righteousness, and I will direct all his ways: he shall build my city, and he shall let go my captives, not for price nor reward, saith the Lord of hosts" (Isaiah 44:28; 45:1,13).

The Decree of Cyrus

It seems clear that what was contemplated was the restoration of the city of Jerusalem as well as of the Temple, and the return of the captives. The actual decree Cyrus promulgated is cited in the last few verses of 2 Chronicles. These words, by which he put the prophecy into effect, are repeated in Ezra 1:1-3 in slightly extended form, where they read as follows:

"Now in the first year of Cyrus king of Persia, that the word of the Lord by the mouth of Jeremiah might be fulfilled, the Lord stirred up the spirit of Cyrus king of Persia, that he made a proclamation throughout all his kingdom, and put it also in writing, saying, Thus saith Cyrus king of Persia, The Lord God of heaven hath given me all the kingdoms of the earth; and he hath charged me to build him an house at Jerusalem, which is in Judah. Who is there among you of all his people? his God be with him, and let him go up to Jerusalem, which is in Judah, and build the house of the Lord God of Israel, (he is the God,) which is in Jerusalem" (see also Ezra 6:3-5).

This, the first decree, was dated the 1st year of Cyrus, approximately A.D. 538. (There is a little variation amongst the "authorities" for the Persian period, usually amounting to one or two years.) However, we are told that "the people of the land" frustrated the efforts of Zerubbabel and Jeshua all the days of Cyrus (Ezra 4:5). The work was resumed in the second year of Darius Hystaspes, 520 B.C., by his decree, and finished in his sixth year (Ezra 4:24; 5:1-2; 6:8-12,14-15).

It may be taken for granted that a good number of people had already established themselves in homes in the area of Jerusalem. The Temple would not be built in a no-man's land; so the decree of Cyrus need not be understood as limited to the construction of the Temple. Ezra himself went up to Judaea by decree, in the 7th year of Artaxerxes (Ezra 7:7-8,11-13,21), 457 B.C. Nehemiah was concerned with the reproach to the Jews of the broken down walls and gates, and the lack of protection (Nehemiah 2:1,5-8,11,17). There were clearly people living in Jerusalem, because when they got down to work, a number of the workers are said, in chapter 3, to have been building the wall nearest to their homes. Nehemiah went up to Jerusalem in the 20th year of Artaxerxes, A.D. 444, but the word "decree" does not appear to be used in this instance.

Calculating 490 years from these starting points on the solar scale, we have the following results:

1st Cyrus	538 B.C.—48 B.C.
2nd Darius Hystaspes	520 B.C.—30 B.C.
7th Artaxerxes	457 B.C.—A.D. 34
20th Artaxerxes	444 B.C.—A.D. 47

Now, it is a matter of history that the "cutting off" of Messiah was about 490 years later than these decrees. A literal application of 70 weeks not making sense, we are forced to count a "week" as seven years in harmony with the symbolism of time periods. The first seven weeks, that is 49 years (Daniel 9:25), includes the period of Ezra for 13 years, then in company with Nehemiah. During these years the people of Israel were re-established in their land and the temple and Jerusalem rebuilt despite opposition from the Samaritans.

Much of the long succeeding 62 weeks was also very troublesome as the next vision will reveal. Nehemiah had two periods in Israel; the second one is dated the 32nd year of Artaxerxes. Pusey calculates that he lived till the 11th of Darius Nothus, thus accounting for 45 of the 49 years of "troublous times" with the Samaritans, counting from the 7th of Artaxerxes.

Messiah "cut off"

Although there is no direct reference to this prophecy in the Gospels, it seems from two indirect references that the Jews understood the period of the prophecy in reference to the Messiah to be currently expiring, for we read in Luke 3:15 concerning the fact that John was baptizing, that "the people were in expectation, and all men mused in their hearts of John, whether he were the Christ or not". The Pharisees tackled John directly on the subject: "Why baptizest thou then, if thou be not *that Christ*, nor Elias, neither that prophet?" (John 1:25). John had to disclaim the honour, but it shows that an expectation of the Messiah (or Christ) was current.

Sixty-two weeks after the first seven there would be one week in the midst of which Messiah would be "cut off". The Hebrew word used here is *karat*, which is the word used for making (literally "cutting") a covenant, as Abraham did—recorded in Genesis 15:10,18.

The first two decrees mentioned above fall short of the appearance of Jesus upon the earth. The third commenced with Ezra going up to Jerusalem with authority in the first month of the year. He therefore received the decree during the passover month and, from that time, 490 solar years would extend to Passover A.D. 34.

Jesus was crucified at Passover time, so here is a way of marking off the years. Jesus began his ministry at about 30 years of age, and it is generally conceded that at his crucifixion he was about 33½ years old. The *Encyclopedia Britannica* puts the crucifixion at A.D. 29, or 30.[3]

The last week of the 70 could be illustrated thus:

A.D.	26	27	28	29	30	31	32	33	34
Age	30	30½	31½	32½	33½				

Because Jesus died "in the midst" of the last 7 years of the period, his birth must therefore have been earlier than B.C. 1.[4] This can be illustrated thus:

B.C.	5	4	3	2	1	1	10	30	A.D.
Age	0	½	1½	2½	3½	4½	13½	33½	

If Jesus was crucified in A.D. 29, the B.C. date for his birth would be correspondingly earlier. King Herod is said to have died in 4 B.C., so Jesus must have been born before then, anything from a few months up to two years (Matthew 2:16). It is noteworthy that if the period is calculated by lunar years (and the Jewish Passover and therefore the crucifixion depended upon the moon), the same number of years, counting 354 days per year, from the later 20th year of Artaxerxes (444 B.C.), ends at almost exactly the same time as the solar calculation from his seventh year.

We have already noted slight variation among authorities for the dates of the Persian period; the uncertainty about the birth year of Jesus creates equal uncertainty about the year of his crucifixion. We cannot therefore be too definitive about the chronology. No doubt there is an *exact* date figure for the fulfilment of the prophecy in the mind of God, and time may reveal it more accurately. In the meantime, with these uncertainties, we are not justified in making a dogmatic decision; even so, the event clearly fulfilled the terms of the prophecy.

The prophecy says the cutting off was to happen "in the midst of the week". Does that mean on the mathematically exact middle day of the last seven years of the period? The Hebrew for "midst", *chatsi*, seems

3. *Encyclopedia Britannica*, in an article "Crucifixion", says Pilate crucified Christ A.D. 32. See *The Christadelphian*, April 1935, for discussion on the subject.
4. This is accounted for by the fact that a chronological error was made by Dionysius Exiguus, who made up the A.D. dates over 500 years after the birth of Christ. Archbishop Ussher calculated this to be four years out; others have since maintained that the birth of Christ was 5, 6 or even 8 years B.C. It depends upon the interpretation of the surviving records of the period when Cyrenius, mentioned in Luke 2:2, held office.

to have an elastic interpretation in some passages at any rate. For example, the mount of Olives shall "cleave in the midst". In a few passages it is translated "part"; that being so, the lack of mathematical certainty about the exact date is no obstacle to the true interpretation of the prophecy which was made over 530 years before the event. The crux of it is that the crucifixion would fall during, or in the middle of, the last of the 70 weeks of years.[5]

The Covenant "confirmed"

What event marks the full ending of the 490 years? The terms of the prophecy are that "he shall confirm the covenant with many for one week" (verse 27). The word "confirm" here is not the usual one meaning to establish or give validity to, but it means *to strengthen*. The R.S.V. reads, "make a strong covenant with many"; Rotherham, in a note, has "strengthen"; Pusey, "make firm a covenant". The use of the Hebrew word *gabar* seems to mean, "He caused to strengthen". The only other occurrence in the same conjugation is Psalm 12:4, "With our tongue will we *prevail*", as though the tongue was an additional agency. Other instances in a different conjugation may be helpful. Ecclesiastes 10:10, "If the iron be blunt, and he do not whet the edge, then must he put to *more strength*". Also Zechariah 10:6,12, "I will *strengthen* the house of Judah ... I will strengthen them in the Lord; and they shall walk up and down in his name". There are other instances also, which suggest that the idea is that something is exerted more than normally.

The use of this word, and the fact that the Passover and Crucifixion were followed in seven weeks by Pentecost, when Jesus' promise of the bestowal of the Holy Spirit was fulfilled to Jewish believers as described in Acts 2, leads to the suggestion that this was an additional strength added to the covenant which had been ratified in the blood of Christ.

The bestowal of the same power upon Cornelius and his fellow-Gentiles would constitute an apt conclusion to this "strengthening of

5. H. Grattan Guinness, *The Approaching End of the Age*, p. 519,524. It had to be a Passover date; Ezra started from Babylon on Passover in 7th of Artaxerxes (Ezra 7:9). Guinness calculates the period to have equalled 6000 lunations less 41-42 days, which shortfall he reckons—including Christ's sleep in the tomb and the time he subsequently spent with his disciples—made exactly 6000 lunations to his ascension. Nehemiah also received his instructions in the Passover month (Nehemiah 2:1). See Guinness, *Light for the Last Days*, 1917 edn., pp. 65-67

THE PROPHECY OF DANIEL

the covenant'' by the later ministration of the Holy Spirit to the Gentiles also. The suggestion is, therefore, that the end of the "week" was marked by this latter event. There is no way of determining the exact date of the conversion of Cornelius described in Acts 10, but some students place it after the conversion of Saul, A.D. 30, or a little later, so that it *could* have been at about the right time for the conclusion of that "week" of years.

The duration of the 70-year Jewish captivity is thus repeated seven times; the last seventy of the 490 years being, as it were, a sabbath, witnessing near its close the advent of our Lord Jesus Christ, the Messiah. The fulfilment of the six clauses by the "cutting off" of Messiah, "though there is nothing against him" (Berkeley), caused the necessity for sacrifice and oblation to cease. The veil of the Temple was rent from top to bottom, and types and shadows became obsolete. It only remained for the destructive forces to arrive, to make the offerings impossible, to cause the overspreading of abominations, and for the desolation to ensue, *until*—in God's own good time—"until the consummation, and that determined shall be poured upon the desolator" (verse 27).

The Apostles of Jesus were witnesses of the exciting events that commenced this process at the Roman destruction in A.D. 70; may we be among those who shall witness its consummation, the destruction of the desolator.

"O Lord, how long?"

CHAPTER 9: APPENDIX I

The Translation of Verse 24

In verse 24 some translators add to the word "Holy" either "place" or "one"; but such a procedure is an *interpretation*, not a translation. If we read "place", it has to be admitted that the "holy place" in Jerusalem was *not* anointed, but destroyed at the expiry of the time period involved; and if the prophecy is falsified, Jesus of Nazareth could not have been the Messiah.

The writer on Daniel in the *Speaker's Commentary*, after comparing the two views concludes, "The phrase is here an attribute of a person". In an excursus in the same work he adds the following: "Others on the contrary, take the words to be the technical phrase for the altar, or the sanctuary, or the temple when anointed; and assert that the phrase is never applied to a person, but always to things. The assertion requires qualification. The phrase is distinctly applied to Aaron (1 Chronicles 23:13); and if the Greek versions are allowed weight here, they distinctly understood the words in dispute in a personal sense ... The LXX when translating (from the Hebrew) 'the Sanctuary' etc. always inserts the article; and the absence of the article here is very significant of the personal sense in which that version took the original Hebrew." Pusey (quoted in the text) also adds his testimony in this sense, saying of the clause in question, "It cannot be spoken of the natural 'holy of holies', which, in contrast to *the holy place*, is always '*the holy of holies*', never '*holy of holies*'. Still less is it the material temple, as a whole, since the temple, as a whole, is never called by the name of a part of it".

Some expositors have cut off the last week of years from the period and placed it at some unspecified date in the remote future. This view was condemned by John Thomas.[1] Bullinger does this in his *Companion Bible*; first because he is unable to accept that the six clauses were fulfilled in the crucifixion, and secondly because he cannot fit his own scheme of chronology with the facts.[2] Others have also adopted

---

1. *The Christadelphian*, 1892, p. 66
2. *The Companion Bible*, Appendix 91

101

a similar interpretation, but if a period of time means anything, it must mean a *consecutive* period; otherwise, by splitting up the period with a long undefined hiatus, it could be made to fulfil one's own predilections in any way.

CHAPTER 9: APPENDIX II

The Word "Weeks"

It has been said that the original word for "weeks" simply means "sevens" and may mean seven of anything. If the prophecy is to have a Christian application, however, the historic facts unavoidably necessitate seventy *sevens of years*, that is, seventy sevens of days, symbolizing 490 years on the day-for-a-year principle. No other application makes sense.

The fact is that though the Hebrew word *shabua* means "a seven", it invariably relates to seven *days*. Thus it is the only word translated "week" in the Old Testament; there is no other. It occurs in this sense 19 times, most of which may be taken literally. The only other way a week is indicated is when it is expressed by different Hebrew words literally as "seven days". In Numbers 28:16-17,26, we have both expressions parallel; and in Ezekiel 45:21, the word *shabua* is itself translated "seven days", so that "week" is a fair translation. *Shabua* is never translated by any other word or phrase.

CHAPTER 10

POOR Daniel! Yet again he is afflicting himself. Why? Two years earlier he had heard the proclamation of Cyrus, and probably had personally witnessed the departure of a company of Jews, led by Sheshbazzar, who carried back to Jerusalem the sacred gold and silver vessels which had been stolen from the Temple by Nebuchadnezzar (Ezra 1:7-11). They were accompanied by Jeshua son of Jozadak the High Priest and his fellows, and also Zerubbabel son of Shealtiel,[1] and other leading Jews. There was every reason for great joy. On arrival, the Jews first built an altar and re-established the morning and evening sacrifices (Ezra 3:1-2). In the second month of the second year after their arrival, they laid the foundation of the Temple (Ezra 3:9-10). The Samaritans, however, resentful at the rejection of their offers of cooperation, frustrated their efforts all the days of Cyrus, and of his son, and the building was not resumed until the second year of Darius Hystaspes in 520 B.C.

Daniel must have heard of this frustration, for it is in the third year of Cyrus that we find him mourning and fasting and preparing himself before God. God is as prompt as He was in responding to his earlier supplication recorded in chapter 9. It is the first month; so from the 14th/15th day onward was Passover week. Daniel fasted for 21 days. Just after the Passover celebration was concluded, on the 24th day Daniel had another and final vision which apparently set his mind at rest (verses 4,12,19).

Daniel's Third Vision

As hinted in chapter 2, the vision Daniel experienced (verses 4-6) was a spiritual contrast to the dream of Nebuchadnezzar, where the image of a man symbolises the kingdoms of men during the whole of their existence. Daniel now sees a MAN who is the antithesis of all this. Daniel's companions fled in fear, just as Paul's companions so long afterwards were filled with fear when Jesus intervened on the way to Damascus. Daniel was left alone; no fleshly element disturbed his spiritual experience. He saw a spiritual symbolic man, which is a

---

1. It is probable that Zerubbabel was another name for Sheshbazzar

collective concept of the MAN God has been calling and electing all through the ages, to become by association with the Messiah, His "peculiar people", to be partakers of the divine nature, who will rule the world on His principles during the Millennium, and people it forever afterwards.

The succession of metals and beasts is only an unhappy interlude, providing a foil for the training of God's own people. John Thomas only touches lightly on this spiritual Man in his *Exposition of Daniel*, but this is probably because in his earlier work *Phanerosis* he had already devoted about 25 pages to an exposition of what he calls "the shadowy representation of 'The Man of the One Eternal Spirit'."

Before going into detail about this symbolic Man, consider the effect of the vision upon Daniel himself. Although this vivid vision is apparently brought into the foreground, like the substance of chapter 8, it is not to materialise for a very long time: not until after "the resurrection" in fact. So for a second time we see Daniel the subject of a symbolic death and resurrection (verses 8-9, cf. 8:18). There are other Scriptural examples of this way of conveying the idea that the dénouement of the vision will not become operative until after the time of resurrection and exaltation to the immortal nature; e.g. Abraham (Genesis 15) and John (Revelation 1).

"Therefore", said Daniel, "I was left alone, and saw this great vision, and there remained no strength in me: for my comeliness was turned in me into corruption, and I retained no strength. Yet heard I the voice of his words: and when I heard the voice of his words, then was I in a deep sleep on my face, and my face toward the ground" (10:8,9).

The praise Daniel received as he is raised to his knees, sets him forth as a great example to the reader. He is greatly beloved. He set his heart to understand, and he chastened himself. His attitude endeared him to God. He could not "understand" without devoting much time and thought to the Word of God and absorbing His thoughts. The great temptation of these days is to give time to the attractive purveyor of *men's* thoughts, the television; and doing without it would be one way of chastening ourselves, and in fact eliminating *anything* that causes our eye, hand or foot to lead us into displeasing God (Matthew 18:8-9).

It is noteworthy that whilst Daniel was in his deathlike sleep, he could *still* hear the voice of the symbolic man. Reference is also made in verses 10-12 to a *hand* that touched him, the owner of which proceeds

THE PROPHECY OF DANIEL

to explain the situation to Daniel. Although no name is mentioned, it seems a fair inference that it was the same hand that touched him and was the same interpreter, as in the two previous visions—the angel Gabriel (8:16; 9:21-23). As before, the speaker says "the vision is for many days" and concerns what is to befall Daniel's people "in the latter days".

Even after being raised to his feet, Daniel is still speechless (verses 15-16), so the "man" touched his lips, indicating that his lips are hallowed by submission to the Word of God, and we can rely on what he says. Isaiah (6:7) and Jeremiah (1:9) both had similar experiences. Verses 15-18 indicate that the resurrection was not immediate— although aroused from sleep Daniel was still weak and dumb—so we are led to conclude that the resurrection is a gradual process. It is possible that the division of the description of the process into two sections, with the comment of verse 19, indicates the intervening judgement:

"Then there came again and touched me one like the appearance of a man, and he strengthened me, and said, O man greatly beloved, fear not: peace be unto thee, be strong, yea, be strong. And when he had spoken unto me, I was strengthened, and said, Let my Lord speak; for thou hast strengthened me."

The narrating angel also inserts into his conversation with Daniel at this juncture one or two of his political activities which can conveniently be considered in a later section. The whole of chapters 10 to 12 constitute one vision, and our Bibles fairly neatly divide it into three parts.

We will now take a closer look at

The Vision of the Man of the One Spirit (verses 4-6)

"In the four and twentieth day of the first month, as I was by the side of the great river, which is Hiddekel; then I lifted up mine eyes, and looked, and behold a certain man clothed in linen, whose loins were girded with fine gold of Uphaz: his body was like the beryl, and his face as the appearance of lightning, and his eyes as lamps of fire, and his arms and his feet like in colour to polished brass, and the voice of his words like the voice of a multitude."

The scene of the vision was on the banks of the river Hiddekel, another name for the Tigris which runs alongside the river Euphrates within the Mesopotamian valley. Assuming Daniel to be normally

106

resident in Babylon, he would have travelled about 50 miles. The phrase "a certain man" is given a marginal alternative rendering "One Man"; comparison should be made with Daniel 7:9 and Revelation 1:12-17.

1. *Clothed in linen:* Nakedness and iniquity are convertible terms. Biblically, to be clothed is to be righteous and holy. White linen was the garb of the priests and represented the righteousness of saints (cf. Revelation 4:4; 19:8,14). It is the figure employed by Jesus in his warning to us, "Behold, I come as a thief. Blessed is he that watcheth, and keepeth his garments, lest he walk naked, and they see his shame" (Revelation 16:15).

2. *Girded with fine gold:* Gold is refined in the fire and represents the *faith* of the believer which is tried in the fire of tribulation, and so is a constituent part of the garb of the Bride of Christ (Psalm 45:9,13). As Peter writes, "Grief in all kind of trials" has come "so that your faith—of greater worth than gold, which perishes even though refined by fire—may be proved genuine and may result in praise, glory and honour when Jesus Christ is revealed" (1 Peter 1:7, N.I.V.).

3. *His body was like the beryl:* There are many organs in one body— it represents a unity of many functions (cf. 1 Corinthians 12:12). Thus we read in Ephesians 4:4, "There is one body, and one spirit, even as ye are called in one hope of your calling"; also in 1:22-23, that God hath put all things under the feet of Jesus "and gave him to be the head over all things to the church, which is his body, the fulness of him that filleth all in all". The Hebrew for beryl is *tarshish*. It was one of the stones in the Aaronic breastplate and corresponded with the tribe of Dan. That name meaning Judgement, is extended in Dan*iel*, to mean judgement of God; and are not his visions heavy with judgement? The beryl therefore symbolises a priestly community in which is incarnated the spirit of the Eternal God. It is also connected with the wheels of Ezekiel's cherubim, and with the "Ancient of Days" (Daniel 7). *Tarshish* is said to be derived from a root meaning to break in pieces, to destroy. This God-manifestation is represented as a consuming fire, and therefore as the antithesis of sin.

4. *His face as the appearance of lightning:* By its expression the face reveals the individual's mood. The Hebrew usually employs the plural form, faces; the Psalmist describes graphically as "smoke out of the nostrils", and "fire out of his mouth", the means by which God destroys His enemies. "Yea, he sent out his arrows, and scattered them; and he shot out lightnings, and discomfited them" (see Psalm 18:8-16; also 2 Thessalonians 1:7-9; Zechariah 9:14).

5. His eyes as lamps of fire: Eyes are the symbols of intelligence and knowledge. The four cherubic "living ones" of Revelation 5:6 are "full of eyes", representing once again the multiple character of the symbolic man who constitutes the Redeemed. The idea is introduced into the dramatisations of Zechariah. In Zechariah 3:8-9 the "stone" which was laid before the High Priest representative of the BRANCH, contained seven eyes; and God says concerning it, that He would engrave the graving thereof Himself, with the ultimate result that He would "remove the iniquity of that land in one day". God's character is reproduced in His Messiah Son, who has complete unity of will with His creator. Harmoniously with Daniel's visions, the ultimate object is the removal of iniquity and the salvation of the saints. Again, in Zechariah 4:10, while they are building the temple, God uses the "plummet" in the hands of Zerubbabel to teach the same lesson, for it carries "those seven; they are the eyes of the Lord, which run to and fro through the whole earth". As verse 6 says, the word is accomplished "not by might, nor by power, but by my spirit, saith the Lord of Hosts". It is by God's power alone, no flesh-power, that His purpose will be consummated. His sight is very penetrating.

6. His arms and his feet like polished brass: The limbs stand for power and strength: "Behold, the Lord God will come with strong hand, and his arm shall rule for him: behold his reward is with him, and his work before him" (Isaiah 40:10). "Awake, awake, put on strength, O arm of the Lord; awake, as in the ancient days" (51:9). "The Lord hath made bare his holy arm in the eyes of all the nations; and all the ends of the earth shall see the salvation of our God" (52:10). The use of the feet is illustrated by Joshua's captains of the army, who placed their feet on the necks of captive kings (Joshua 10:24)—an action commemorated by David in Psalm 18:32-40.

In Scripture brass is associated with the court of the tabernacle, with the covering of the altar of burnt offering, etc.; that is, with the outer furnishings, not with the interior of the holy place or most holy. So the spiritual man tramples on the old Adam nature which is manifested by the impulses of the natural man. He "puts off the old man", and "puts on the new man" (Ephesians 4:24). This is the meaning of the appeal of Jesus, "Take up the cross, and follow me" (Mark 10:21). Taking

up the cross is a voluntary action exemplifying the crucifixion of
Jesus; not a resigned acceptance of some pain or trouble that might
happen to anyone (Matthew 16:24-28). All this is implied in the fact
that the arms and feet of the One Man, are of *polished* brass. The brass
(or bronze) is not left in its natural state, but is *worked upon*. This
symbol is rare in Scripture: only four instances in all. The cherubim
of Ezekiel 1:7 had feet that "sparkled like ... *burnished* brass"
(the same Hebrew as "polished", *qalal*). The Apocalyptic counterpart
calls it "*fine*" brass, which looked as though it glowed in a furnace
(Revelation 1:15; 2:18).

Isaiah refers to the power and strength of God's arm, in bringing
salvation:

"He saw that there was no man, and wondered that there was no
intercessor: therefore his arm brought salvation unto him; and his
righteousness, it sustained him. For he put on righteousness as a
breastplate, and an helmet of salvation upon his head; and he put on
the garments of vengeance for clothing, and was clad with zeal as a
cloke ... And the Redeemer shall come to Zion, and unto them that
turn from transgression in Jacob, saith the LORD. As for me, this is
my covenant with them, saith the LORD; My spirit that is upon thee,
and my words which I have put in thy mouth, shall not depart out
of thy mouth, nor out of the mouth of thy seed, nor out of the mouth
of thy seed's seed, saith the LORD, from henceforth and for ever"
(59:16-17,20-21).

The aged Daniel must have been very comforted with the thought of
awakening once more to undergo the change to the divine nature which
he saw symbolized before him; to becoming a part of the Man of the
One Spirit to rule the world with Jesus in the Kingdom of God, instead
of having to steer a difficult course in the service of such men as
Nebuchadnezzar and Cyrus.

If these things are written for our learning, we too must try in
our imagination to relive the experience with Daniel, and appropriate
to ourselves the comfort the visions afford, for the end of another
age is upon *us*, and so much more has transpired to bring us nearer
our desired haven. We did not see Jesus either transfigured or
crucified, but we have vivid accounts in the Scripture of these events
which we must allow to live in our minds, with the anticipation of
"the Son of Man coming in the clouds of heaven with power and great
glory".

Michael

Although the burden of this vision concerns the far distant future, the narrating angel commences with references to contemporary history. It seems to be characteristic of these visions concerning the development of world events, to detail the early stages, and then to describe the later stages either in vaguer terms or in a more compact form, so that a few sentences cover ages of time.

As a preliminary to the narration in chapter 11 we gather together the substance of verses 12, 13 and 20-21 of chapter 10:

"From the first day that thou didst set thine heart to understand, and to chasten thyself before thy God, thy words were heard, and I am come for thy words. But the prince of the kingdom of Persia withstood me one and twenty days: but, lo, Michael, one of the chief princes, came to help me; and I remained there with the kings of Persia . . . Knowest thou wherefore I come unto thee? and now will I return to fight with the prince of Persia: and when I am gone forth, lo, the prince of Grecia shall come. But I will shew thee that which is noted in the scripture of truth: and there is none that holdeth with me in these things, but Michael your prince."

It appears, then, that while Daniel was fasting three weeks, the "hand" angel that touched him (Gabriel ?), was at the same time being withstood by the prince of Persia. Hitherto harmony had existed between them, and Cyrus had done the right thing. What was he doing now? History books do not seem to help much at this point. But since it says "prince" rather than "king" of Persia, perhaps it was what Cyrus' son and vice-regent Cambyses was doing, that was the trouble.[2] Still, it does not appear that Cyrus himself did anything further to implement his own decree, with the result that the Temple building was delayed for 21 years (538-516). "Michael, one of the chief princes, came to help me; and I remained there with the kings of Persia" (verse 13). The use of the plural for "kings" here, seems to show that this was not a matter of a very short time, but extends beyond the life-time of Daniel himself, and perhaps of Cyrus and his successors.

Who was Michael? The meaning of the name is given as "Who like God", which may be more freely understood in English as "Who is like God". He is said to be "one of the chief princes" (verse 13), and to Daniel he is described as "your prince" (verse 21). In chapter 12:1

---

2. It might also be the unnamed opponents of Zerubbabel that are involved, since they also would be the officials of the Persian regime.

he is described as "the great prince which standeth for the children of thy people", that is of the Jews. He seems to be identifiable with the angel God appointed to lead Moses: "Behold, I send an Angel before thee, to keep thee in the way, and to bring thee into the place which I have prepared ... my name is in him ... for mine Angel shall go before thee ..." (Exodus 23:20-23). Later, Joshua saw what he thought was a man with a drawn sword in his hand. Upon challenging him Joshua is told, "As captain of the host of the Lord am I now come" (Joshua 5:14-15). These divine manifestations are not named, but it seems a reasonable inference that it was the same angelic being throughout.

In the Epistle of Jude he *is* named in verse 9: "Yet Michael the archangel, when contending with the devil he disputed about the body of Moses, durst not bring against him a railing accusation, but said, The Lord rebuke thee." This is a direct reference to what was going on in Israel at the very epoch we are considering. When the Samaritans were in opposition to Zerubbabel, Ezra, Jeshua the High priest and Zechariah the prophet, the situation was dramatised in Zechariah chapter 3: "And he shewed me Joshua the high priest standing before the angel of the LORD, and Satan standing at his right hand to resist him. And the LORD said unto Satan, The LORD rebuke thee, O Satan: even the LORD that hath chosen Jerusalem rebuke thee: is not this a brand plucked out of the fire?" (verses 1,2). Israel was the "body of Moses", just as spiritual Israel is the "body of Christ", as has already been exhibited in the Man of the One Spirit. And so, in spite of opposition, with the help of God, the work went on. As the work of rebuilding proceeded in Jerusalem in the time of Jeshua the son of Jozadak, so the greater Joshua is active on behalf of spiritual Israel in our own day.

CHAPTER 11

DANIEL's Third Vision continues into this chapter and on into chapter 12. After seeing the vision of the symbolic Man, Daniel was told of the angel's struggle to control these earthly rulers. There is no recourse to the earlier symbolic language concerning a ram and a goat; instead Daniel is told in plain language about the Persians, and of the appearance of the prince of Greece. With the opening of chapter 11 the angel recapitulates, referring back to his initial success with Darius the Mede (Cyrus?), before explaining the coming succession of Persian kings, their eventual defeat at the hands of Alexander the Greek, and the subsequent development, previously noted symbolically by four horns growing up upon the goat in place of the great horn which had been broken.

The prophecy that follows has been so precisely fulfilled in history that sceptics have claimed it was written after the event. We have already seen that the book of Daniel appears in the LXX version, so the prophecy must have been already in existence well before Ptolemy Philadelphus (if it was he) had it translated for his library about 286 B.C. Had it been a later production the names of the principal characters would undoubtedly have been cited.

The details of the prophecy may seem superfluous to us when compared with the compact definition of the Man image and the various beasts. Although the Word is recorded and preserved for our admonition, upon whom the end of the age has come (1 Corinthians 10:11), we must think of the needs of the Jews, both those who had returned to Israel under Zerubbabel and those who remained as the *diaspora* (dispersed) during the centuries before Christ. To have been able to watch the outworking of this prophecy year after year, must surely have been both a comfort and a warning to generation after generation of any who had eyes to see, and ears to hear, and to be attentive to what the prophets of God had recorded on His behalf. The record is sufficiently literal for all the main features of political developments to be identified as time passed by.

The Persian Régime

Verse 2: "There shall stand up yet three kings in Persia; and the fourth shall be far richer than they all". After Cyrus, the next of the three rulers was his son Cambyses (529-521 B.C.). He is reputed to have murdered his brother Smerdis, to have conquered Egypt and later to have gone mad. It appears that a sham "Smerdis" otherwise known as Gomates, Gautama or pseudo-Smerdis was proclaimed king. Cambyses set out to quell the rebellion, but died suddenly on the way. After a reign of seven months Gomates was pursued and killed by a cousin of Cambyses, Darius son of Hystaspes who then became king (521-485 B.C.).

The fourth and richer king was Xerxes I (485-465 B.C.) who is very probably the Ahasuerus served by Mordecai, and who married Esther. "By his strength through his riches he shall stir up all against the realm of Grecia." Several other Persian kings are passed over unnoticed in the text.

The next to reign was Artaxerxes Longimanus who was the one Nehemiah served; but it was Xerxes who first started the war with Greece and that is the concern of chapter 11. Concerning Xerxes we are told that immediately upon his accession he began to make preparation for the invasion of Greece. Two of the greatest works he performed were the cutting of a canal through the isthmus of Mt. Athos and the bridging of the Hellespont.

The expedition, however, was not a success and Xerxes had to return precipitately into Asia, his fleet having been destroyed; but its huge extent is indicative of his riches and the use to which he put them. His invasion started a war which lasted during the careers of several subsequent rulers in Persia.

Verse 3, a model of brevity, prophesies that "a mighty king shall stand up, that shall rule with great dominion, and do according to his will". This was undoubtedly the Greek king Alexander, who ascended the Greek throne in 336 B.C. In 334 he utterly defeated the Persians on the banks of the river Granicus in Mysia. Later he defeated the Persian forces under Darius III at Issus in Cilicia. After conquering Syria and Egypt, he again advanced against Persia, and in 331 B.C. he won the decisive victory of Gaugamela over an army reputed to be of one million men. Babylon and Susa at once submitted and he went on to reach India. He died still a young man in 323 B.C.

113

THE PROPHECY OF DANIEL

The Grecian Régime

Verse 4: "And when he shall stand up, his kingdom shall be broken, and shall be divided toward the four winds of heaven; and not to his posterity, nor according to his dominion which he ruled: for his kingdom shall be plucked up, even for others beside those." The empire was not inherited by any descendant or relative of Alexander. For 20 years Alexander's generals fought over the sub-division of the Empire, which eventually settled down after the battle of Ipsus in 301 B.C., into the fourfold division predicted. Very briefly, Cassander occupied Greece, Lysimachus was located in Asia Minor, Ptolemy in Egypt, and Seleucus in Syria. The struggle did not end there, however, for in another 20 years the four were reduced to two; and henceforth we read in the text of "the king of the south" and "the king of the north."

The Kings of the South and of the North

Seleucus Nicator assumed the role of king of the north, taking possession of the Asiatic provinces. The role of the king of the south was headed by Ptolemy Soter, who controlled Egypt and adjacent territories, which included Palestine. For some time there was frequent war between these two, which ended in the murder of Seleucus Nicator by Ceraunus, one of Ptolemy's sons. Nicator's son Antiochus Soter, reigning from 280 to 261 B.C., suffered a series of misfortunes and was defeated and slain by the Gauls. This king of the north was succeeded by his son Antiochus Theos, who reigned from 261 to 247 B.C. He was a base character, and his only triumphs were in war with Egypt. This war was brought to an end by a treaty of marriage. The king of the south, Ptolemy Soter, abdicated in favour of his youngest son Ptolemy Philadelphus (285-247 B.C.). It was he who after much war with Syria acted out the fulfilment of verse 6, together with Antiochus Theos:

Verse 6: "And in the end of years they shall join themselves together; for the king's daughter of the south shall come to the king of the north to make an agreement." The daughter of Ptolemy Philadelphus was Berenice. Antiochus Theos on his part repudiated his former wife Laodice, and contracted the agreement with Philadelphus. However, the prophecy says, "but she shall not retain the power of the arm". This refers to her father, for when he died, Antiochus Theos put Berenice away and recalled his former wife. But the text goes on, "Neither shall he (the king of the north) stand, nor his arm: but she shall be given up, and they that brought her, and he that begat her, and

114

he that strengthened her in these times.'' Laodice, on her return to favour, treacherously poisoned her husband Antiochus. Berenice and her son were then at her mercy; history says she did this to secure the throne for her son, Seleucus Callinicus. The two, as might have been expected, compassed the death of Berenice and her son, thus fulfilling to the letter verse 7.

Verse 7: ''But out of a branch of her roots shall one stand up in his estate''. This branch of her roots was her brother, Ptolemy Euergetes (247-222 B.C.), the son of her father Ptolemy Philadelphus. Verse 7 continues: ''. . . which shall come with an army, and shall enter into the fortress of the king of the north, and shall deal against them, and shall prevail.'' In this way did Euergetes avenge his sister's death. He invaded and conquered Syria, and then withdrew into Egypt with much spoil:

Verse 8: ''(He) shall also carry captives into Egypt their gods, with their princes, and with their precious vessels of silver and of gold . . . So the king of the south shall come into his kingdom and shall return into his own land.'' Seleucus Callinicus however escaped; he recovered his provinces, but died in war, falling from his horse while still a young man, about 226 B.C., so that as Ptolemy Euergetes reigned until 222 B.C., he further fulfilled verse 8, as he ''continued more years than the king of the north''.

Verse 10: ''But his (Callinicus') sons shall be stirred up, and shall assemble a multitude of great forces: and one shall certainly come, and overflow, and pass through: then shall he return, and be stirred up, even to his fortress.'' The sons of Callinicus were Seleucus Ceraunus (226-223 B.C.), and Antiochus the Great (223-187). This latter, evidently the ''one'' referred to in this verse, made war with the king of the south, ''overflowing and passing through''. He met with initial success but subsequently sustained defeat on all hands, and ''returned, stirred up even to his fortress''. By this time Ptolemy Euergetes had been succeeded by his son Ptolemy Philopator (222-205). After his initial success, Antiochus returned to winter quarters because of the lateness of the season. In 217 B.C. Ptolemy Philopator marched with a large army to Raphia; Antiochus was again stirred up to war, and, heavily defeated, retreated to his fortress. Philopator advanced again:

Verse 11: ''And the king of the south shall be moved with choler, and shall come forth and fight with him, even with the king of the north.''

He was met by Antiochus who "shall set forth a great multitude; but the multitude shall be given into his hand." The multitude of Antiochus was 72,000 foot-soldiers and 6,000 horse-men, but he suffered severe defeat, having been "given into the hand" of the king of Egypt.

Verse 12: "And when he hath taken away the multitude, his heart shall be lifted up; and he shall cast down many ten thousands: but he shall not be strengthened." He was not strengthened by this victory as Philopator did not follow it up; but, attempting to enter the Holy Place, he was stricken down and died.

Verses 13,14: Nineteen years after the battle of Raphia, Antiochus advanced with another large army: "The king of the north shall return, and shall set forth a multitude greater than the former, and shall certainly come after certain years with a great army and with much riches." That was in 198 B.C. In this venture, Antiochus repossessed Palestine and Coele-Syria and "in those times, there shall many stand up against the king of the south". Philopator, at his death (205 B.C.), was succeeded by his only son Ptolemy Epiphanes, who was just 5 years old. This is the one against whom many were to stand up; it is not surprising that they should thus take advantage of his tender age. Not only was Epiphanes opposed by Antiochus but he was the subject of intrigues in Egypt itself.

We next read, "Also the robbers of thy people shall exalt themselves to establish the vision". "Thy people", are, of course, the Jews; and this first reference to them in this prophecy brings us close to the essence of the vision. It appears that at this stage in history, the Romans interfered in Egyptian affairs under the pretext of affording protection to the juvenile Ptolemy Epiphanes, but without being of much help to him at this time. Who are "the robbers of thy people"[1] in verse 14,

---

1. Young gives the meaning of the original for "robbers" as "breakers in or forth", i.e. burglars; and he renders the phrase "sons of the destroyers of thy people". Rotherham translates, "The sons of the oppressors of thy people will exalt themselves to confirm the vision, but will be overthrown". The question still remains as to whether they are destroyers or violent men belonging to the Jews, as many modern versions render it, or Gentiles oppressing Jews. John Thomas chose the latter interpretation using the word "breakers" instead of "robbers", and applying it to the Romans. The Romans unconsciously fulfilled the vision, but were ultimately to fall. The reference to the "vision" puzzles many commentators, but the Spirit's choice of words is never aimless. The Amplified Bible applies it to the vision of Daniel 8:6,9. Others think it has nothing to do with any revelatory book. But the reference must be deliberate, and has to do with the revelation the angel is engaged in conveying to Daniel.

and what vision are they concerned with? Acts 13:27 seems to elucidate the matter: Paul, speaking at Pisidian Antioch, says "For they that dwell at Jerusalem, and their rulers, because they knew him not, nor yet the voices of the prophets which are read every sabbath day, they have fulfilled them in condemning him. And though they found no cause of death in him, yet desired they Pilate that he should be slain". The Romans unconsciously fulfilled the vision, but were ultimately to fall.

Here in Daniel 11:14, we have the first appearance of the Romans upon the scene; the first glimpse of the embryonic "little horn" which was to grow out of one of the four Greek horns.

Verse 15: The ineffectiveness of the Roman help at this juncture is seen when "the king of the north shall come, and cast up a mount, and take the most fenced cities: and the arms of the south shall not withstand, neither his chosen people, neither shall there be any strength to withstand". This is a further reference to the campaign of 198 B.C., by which Antiochus the Great secured Palestine and Coele-Syria, besieging Sidon, capturing Jerusalem, and expelling the Egyptian garrisons.

Verse 16: In the process he devastated the land: "He that cometh against him (i.e. Antiochus), shall do according to his own will, and none shall stand before him: and he shall stand in the glorious land, which by his hand shall be consumed". The "vision" is now centring attention upon the land of Israel, and the Jewish people.

At the time the Romans appointed their deputy in Egypt, they did the same in Greece, proclaiming that country free. Antiochus now turned his attention to Greece, desiring to acquire that territory. In doing so he caused greater displeasure to Rome than ever. This enterprise is outlined in:

Verse 17: "He shall also set his face to enter with the strength of his whole kingdom, and upright ones with him; thus shall he do". As a precautionary measure, he endeavoured to secure the neutrality of Egypt by arranging a marriage treaty. Antiochus gave his daughter Cleopatra in marriage to Ptolemy Epiphanes with a dowry consisting of Coele-Syria and Palestine. The idea was that she should influence the young Ptolemy Epiphanes, who was only 15 years old. She would have her father's interests at heart, and carry this territory as a bribe, half the revenue of which was to go to Antiochus. In this way, "he shall give him the daughter of women, corrupting her". Events did not turn out quite as he had anticipated, however, for "she shall not stand on his side, neither be for him". Cleopatra (not the later one connected with Mark Anthony) sided with her husband Epiphanes. With his expedition against the Grecian islands, Antiochus' successes came to an end, although he had a measure of success at first:

Verse 18: "After this shall he turn his face unto the isles, and shall take many", but the reproach the Romans had previously suffered at his hands in Egypt was turned upon him in Greece, as the later part of the verse describes: "But a prince for his own behalf shall cause the reproach offered by him to cease; without his own reproach he shall cause it to turn upon him". Scipio the Roman consul eventually defeated him and drove him from every part of Asia Minor, imposing a heavy indemnity.

Verse 19: "Then he shall turn his face toward the fort of his own land: but he shall stumble and fall, and not be found". It was in 188 B.C. that he obtained peace with the Romans on condition that he ceded large territory and paid the indemnity. In an attempt to obtain money for this purpose, he robbed a temple at Elymais, and was murdered by the outraged people of the place.

Verse 20: "Then shall stand up in his estate a raiser of taxes in the glory of the kingdom: but within few days he shall be destroyed, neither in anger, nor in battle". Antiochus the Great was succeeded by his son Seleucus Philopator (187-175 B.C.). This man maintained friendly relations with Egypt and Rome, and devoted his energies to gathering money by taxation, with which to pay the Romans. Philopator was poisoned by his minister Heliodorus who acted the part of a usurper. He is the "vile person" of:

Verse 21: "In his estate shall stand up a vile person, to whom they shall not give the honour of the kingdom: but he shall come in peaceably, and obtain the kingdom by flatteries". For a brief time the throne was occupied by the assassin; but Antiochus Epiphanes, a brother of the late king, obtained the throne as the verse says, "by flatteries". The reign of Antiochus Ephiphanes (176-164 B.C.) is minutely detailed in verses 21-31. He conducted a war with Egypt from 171 to 168 B.C. in which he was successful.

Verse 22: "With the arms of a flood shall they be overflown from before him, and shall be broken; yea, also the prince of the covenant".

118

Palestine must have suffered severely during all these campaigns, situated as it is directly between the home territories of the kings of the north and south. In this case Onias the High Priest (the "prince of the covenant") was deposed, detained elsewhere, and later slain in 172 B.C. (a pale shadow of chapter 8:11). This Epiphanes oppressed the Jews and captured Jerusalem in 172 and 168 B.C. The Jews revolted under Mattathias and the Maccabees and defeated Lysias his general. These details are worked out much more fully in the succeeding verses of the prophecy.

The contemporary king of the south was Ptolemy Philometor, son of the Ptolemy Epiphanes of the infant accession; he reigned from 181-146 B.C., although his mother was regent until 173. It was after this that Antiochus Epiphanes commenced his incursions into Egypt. But although conquering most of Egypt, he was unable to take Alexandria. After his second invasion in 170 B.C. Antiochus made a league with Philometor, but he worked deceitfully:

Verse 23: "And after the league made with him he shall work deceitfully, for he shall come up, and shall become strong with a small people". Renewing the war he came to Alexandria and by intrigues peacefully obtained possession of the best provinces of Egypt.

Verse 24: "He shall enter peaceably even upon the fattest places of the province; and he shall do that which his fathers have not done, nor his fathers' fathers"—and that was to divide the spoils among his soldiers; "he shall scatter among them the prey, and spoil, and riches: yea, and he shall forecast his devices against the strong holds, even for a time".

Verse 25: With this measure of success, "he shall stir up his power and his courage against the king of the south with a great army; and the king of the south shall be stirred up to battle with a very great and mighty army; but he shall not stand: for they shall forecast devices against him". Philometor, as was foretold, did not stand. Seeing he was in the hands of Antiochus, the Alexandrians placed his brother Euergetes II upon the throne.

Verse 26: "Yea, they that feed of the portion of his (Philometor's) meat shall destroy him, and his army shall overflow: and many shall fall down slain". Although Philometor was not slain, Antiochus' army spread into Egypt, and many were slain. Antiochus and Euergetes II at length came together, but "both these kings' hearts (were) to do mischief."

119

THE PROPHECY OF DANIEL

Verses 27,28: "And they shall speak lies at one table; but it shall not prosper: for yet the end shall be at the time appointed. Then shall he return into his land with great riches; and his heart shall be against the holy covenant; and he shall do exploits". On his return Antiochus sacked Jerusalem, and taking with him much treasure and many slaves, passed on to Antioch his capital.

Verse 29: Antiochus had yet another excursion to make into Egypt: "At the time appointed he shall return, and come toward the south; but it shall not be as the former, or as the latter". It was under the pretext of restoring Philometor to the throne that Antiochus once more turned his attention to Egypt. He advanced against Alexandria and besieged it, but did not proceed as he had done previously, or would do again; but raising the siege he marched towards Memphis, where he installed Philometor as king. As soon as he had departed, however, Philometor came to an understanding with Euergetes, and they agreed to reign jointly over Egypt. When Antiochus heard of it, he led a powerful army against Memphis, to subdue the country. Having nearly accomplished his project, he marched against Alexandria, which was the only obstacle to his becoming absolute master of Egypt. But the Roman embassy, sent at the request of the Ptolemies, met him about a mile from the city. They had left Rome with the utmost diligence. When they arrived at Delos, they found a fleet of Macedonian or Greek ships in which they embarked for Alexandria, where they arrived as Antiochus approached. Popilius delivered to Antiochus the decree of the Senate, and demanded an immediate answer. Sorely against his will he agreed to obey its mandate, and draw off his army from Egypt. Thus his invasion terminated very differently from the former and the latter. This is the fulfilment of:

Verse 30: "For the ships of Chittim shall come against him (preventing him from incorporating Egypt into his Assyrian dominion): therefore he shall be grieved, and return, and have indignation against the holy covenant: so shall he do; he shall even return, and have intelligence with them that forsake the holy covenant". So in 168 B.C. he vented his spleen on the Jews by placing 20,000 men under Apollonius with orders to destroy Jerusalem. After entering into an alliance with some unfaithful Jews:

Verses 31,32: The army despatched to Jerusalem destroyed most of the city, literally profaned the Temple, suppressing the daily sacrifice; and by placing an idol image of Jupiter Olympius in the Temple

(2 Maccabees 6:2), fulfilled the last clause of verse 31, "and they shall place the abomination that maketh desolate. And such as do wickedly against the covenant shall he corrupt by flatteries". These were the unfaithful Jews, who assisted Antiochus and his men in their devastating work, whilst "the people that do know their God shall be strong, and do exploits".

Those doing the "exploits" doubtless included the Maccabean family who strengthened themselves, and the remainder of the Jews who were faithful to the law. The word "exploits", however, is not in the original. A Jewish Rabbi, Rashi, interprets the word "do" to mean "to keep the law".

Verse 33: The Maccabees were not strong enough to turn away Antiochus and his bands, but suffered oppression and scattering for a time. But it had been prophesied: "When they shall fall, they shall be holpen with a little help".

After this gloomy period of oppression, under the leadership of the Maccabean brothers they began to be more successful, defeating and killing Apollonius and also defeating the general Lysias in two successful encounters. There may have been a supernatural element in this "little help", which could account for several remarkable victories over superior forces. We can imagine the unfaithful Jews returning perhaps shamefacedly to their countrymen. But to cleave to them only by flatteries, as the end of verse 34 states they would do, could not be acceptable in God's sight. Such a condition would require purging, and purging is accomplished by fiery trial. The effect of this is indicated in the next verse:

Verse 35: "Some of them of understanding shall fall, to try them, and to purge, and to make them white, even to the time of the end: because it is yet for a time appointed."

The death of Antiochus Epiphanes took place in A.D. 164, during the "many days" of verse 33. From that point we have no further reference to the kings of the north and south until the later part of the prophecy. It appears that not all religious Jews adopted the rebellious spirit of the Maccabean brothers; some died offering no resistance, others died refusing to defend themselves on the sabbath. Fairweather writes: "Many were, of course, content to conform to Gentile customs in order to save their lives; but the flower of Israel, the energetic men and women who loved their country, were prepared to die rather than renounce their faith. And these were in the majority ... Nothing sifts a nation like persecution; it forces every man to take his side. Those who continued faithful to the law now entered into a solemn league to maintain their sacred institutions. Known at first by the name of the *Chasidim*, or pious ones, and afterwards by that of Pharisees, they soon embraced within their party all that was bravest and best in Israel. Their action had no political significance: the one thing for which they contended was liberty to worship God according to their conscience. So extreme was their regard for the strict letter of the law, that as many as a thousand of them permitted themselves to be butchered by the Syrian soldiers rather than do anything in self-defence on the Sabbath day. But, with all their reluctance to take up arms, these pious men—the Covenanters of that age—soon perceived that they must choose between this and extermination. And so at last, along with all who were like-minded, they took the sword, and 'smote sinful men in their anger, and wicked men in their wrath'."[2]

In spite of the strictures of Jesus, not all Pharisees were bad, and many afterwards became Christians along with other Jewish leaders (John 3:1; 12:42; Acts 6:7). Paul, too, was proud of his association with the Pharisees (Acts 23:6; 26:5); what they needed, in common with everyone else, was *conversion*.

The Alternative View

That is one interpretation of the prophecy. The "Abomination that maketh Desolate" will be dealt with in Appendix I; meanwhile we will outline an alternative application of verses 30-35 of chapter 11.

Noting the intrusion of the Romans into middle-eastern affairs, and that they had for years been encroaching, expanding and absorbing, an alternative view sees in the reference to the "ships of Chittim", by means of which they supported Egypt and prevented Antiochus Epiphanes from accomplishing his purpose of conquering that country, a switch in the subject of the prophecy. So that, instead of the forces of Antiochus Epiphanes being the power that desecrates the temple, it is the Romans who fulfil this part of the prophecy about 200 years later. We have to remember that, taken as a whole, the prophecy is to extend over more than 2000 years, so that we have to think in terms of ages or epochs once we have passed the early detailed part, which benefited those living in the contemporary period.

---

2. Wm. Fairweather, *From the Exile to the Advent*, pp. 128-9

In the course of this expansion, the Roman power had occupied the territory formerly held by Cassander, one of Alexander's four generals, and which had been held briefly and intermittently by the king of the north; Rome eventually absorbed the territory of the kings of the north and south. Roman power therefore prospers during the time of the indignation against Israel. From the time of the absorption of Judea by Pompey, the "indignation" lasts until the time of the end, when it is "accomplished", or brought to an end. Judah will then once again become a holy nation.

According to this view, it is the Romans who desecrate the Temple and install the abomination, in the form of the ensigns of the Roman legions, to which the soldiers offered sacrifices within the precincts of the Temple. Some time after the destruction of the Temple in A.D. 70, the Romans built a new city on the site of Jerusalem, naming it Aelia Capitolina and erected in A.D. 132 a temple to Jupiter on the site of the ruins of Herod's Temple. In this interpretation, the succeeding references to the Jewish people must have a Christian connotation.

Reverting for the moment to the times of Antiochus Epiphanes, Fairweather further comments: "The Maccabean party had been essentially Pharisaic in its origin, and John Hyrcanus was himself a valued disciple of the Pharisees." Hyrcanus was a scion of the Maccabean family, and in the fighting and intrigue of the times he assumed the office of High Priest. "But the relative importance attached by them to political supremacy and religious praxis was gradually bringing about an estrangement between this powerful sect and the reigning High Priest." The upshot was that through an altercation of a personal nature between John Hyrcanus and his Pharisee colleagues, he changed sides; so that the High Priests were henceforth Sadducees, of whom Fairweather comments that "their spirit was as secular as that of the Pharisees was religious".[3] Such people would be subject to the pressures of either Antiochus Epiphanes or the Roman Caesars as verse 32 describes: "And such as do wickedly against the covenant shall he corrupt by flatteries: but the people that do know their God shall be strong, and do."

In interpreting verses 32-35, it would appear that if God determined to put His servants to the test, the *principles* which He would bring to bear would be the same, whether in the Maccabean or in the Christian era. The difference in the Christian dispensation would be that believers

3. Wm. Fairweather, *From the Exile to the Advent*, pp. 158,161

would have to acknowledge that Jesus of Nazareth was the Messiah; they had to choose between light and darkness. As far as verse 32 the emphasis in the text is on "the holy covenant", which in its context would appear to mean the old covenant (the Law). Curiously, although we have much amplification of chapter 8 in chapter 11, there is no reference to Messiah, or of a new covenant. That had already been enlarged upon in chapter 9.

So, applying verses 33-35 to the days of Jesus, the apostles and soon after, it would be easy to cite instances of martyrdom by the sword, by burning, imprisonment and banishment. The "little help" would be evident from many acts of God's providence written and unrecorded which faithful Christians experienced in Apostolic times and after- wards. Purging by persecution and "fiery trial" is a matter of prin- ciple; it is necessary to the "making white" of all faithful disciples, so the prophecy continues, "even to the time of the end: because it is yet for a time appointed". God has the whole matter under control— always—because He rules in the kingdom of men.

The fact that there were *two* desecrations of the Temple, and that the context seems to be capable of either interpretation (though Jesus only refers to the second), suggests that there is a conflation here. Believers living in both epochs can derive stimulus and comfort from reading the prophecy. From *our* point of view, we know that the Roman application was clearly fulfilled in the days of the disciples, and that should surely be the basis of *our* confidence. It is the key to the application of the succeeding passage of a "king", later still in time, located neither north nor south, but identifiable with the "little horn" which grew out of one of the four.

The "little horn" King

Verses 36-39: Following the prophecy of the kings of the north and south, these verses refer to a king whose existence extends from that time right up to "the time of the end". As in previous chapters, therefore, the "king" must be regarded as a kingdom or power, not just a single individual; in fact it must be a series of phases of power, since the period involved extends over more than 2000 years. He must also be identifiable with the "king of fierce countenance" of chapter 8:23-25, whose characteristics may be enumerated as follows:

1. He corresponds with the little horn growing out of one of the four horns of the goat.

2. He understands dark sentences.
3. He is mighty but not by his own power.
4. He destroys wonderfully, including the holy people, the Jews.
5. He causes craft to prosper.
6. He magnifies himself in his heart.
7. He shall destroy many by peace (or prosperity).
8. Finally he opposes Christ, and is destroyed by him.

This power was to arise later than Antiochus Epiphanes, who was a representative of one of the four horns; and it must commence prior to the time of the Saracens, because they did not come into the picture until long after the Grecian empire had been eclipsed by the Romans. When we add the characteristics of the "king" of chapter 11:36, the conclusion that the power that is represented is a phase of Rome seems unavoidable.

The characteristics of the "king" of chapter 11 are:

1. He is wilful.
2. He exalts himself above every god.
3. He speaks against the God of gods.
4. He prospers till the "indignation" is accomplished.
5. He regards not the god of his fathers.
6. Nor the desire of women.
7. He magnifies self above all.
8. He honours a "god of forces", whom his fathers knew not, with gold and precious things. The "god of forces", verse 38, is in A.V. margin Hebrew *mahuzzim*, God's protectors; or as rendered by John Thomas, "a god of guardians".
9. He will divide the land for gain.

As we have seen, the encroaching Roman power took possession of Macedonia which had passed from Antigonus and his son Demetrius to Cassander, and later almost into the hands of Seleucus. Rome finally took Macedonia and Greece in 145 B.C., and then gradually incorporated the rest of the erstwhile Grecian empire, except for the eastern part which was taken by the Parthians. Rome therefore fills the rôle of a little horn growing out of the Macedonian wing of Alexander's empire of the goat (Daniel 8:9), and also of the fourth beast of chapter 7, which succeeded the Greek leopard.

After the suppression of the "holy" and the abolition of the evening-morning sacrifice in A.D. 70, pagan Rome later became Christianized. The "king" changed his gods. Pagan Roman emperors had long adopted the eastern concept of regarding themselves as the divine representative of a god, and demanded worship accordingly. This no faithful Jew or Christian could render—hence the persecution that arose. But with the apostasy of professing Christian men with political ambition, the "king" became able to adopt the apostate form of Christianity, a religion unknown to his fathers, which would be characterized in time by a celibate clergy, and the canonizing of dead "saints", constituting them heavenly intercessors or "guardians". They dedicated churches in their honour, into which were collected and devoted articles of gold and many precious and valuable things, whilst the ordinary people who contributed the substance lived in poverty. The people were ruled through the confessional, and sale of "indulgences", and payment of fees for saying masses for the dead; and the land was divided for gain into parishes. Thus the power wielded was not by armies under their control. Perhaps worst of all was the blasphemous adoption of titles that should have belonged to God alone, and the ultimate claim to "infallibility" by which the Papacy was logically declared to be God, "sitting in the temple of God, showing himself that he is God" (2 Thessalonians 2:4; cf. chapter 7, page 66).

This development was helped forward in the 4th century by the emperor Constantine transferring his capital from Rome to Constantinople (now Istanbul) right into the arena of the previous goat empire, whilst supporting the embryonic Papacy, the bishopric of Rome. Constantine was originally a devotee of Apollo, and as king he was regarded as the apotheosis of Apollo. It appears that as he became influenced by Christians, he simply transferred his divine claims to be the representative of Christ, a claim likewise made by his successors. This kingdom therefore was and remained "catholic", under a Roman dynasty of emperors, until after a long period of affliction by Saracen invaders, it was ultimately brought to an end by the Turkish overflow in A.D. 1453.

Since that time, we have had in the Middle East an Islamic kingdom which lasted about 400 years, before it too gradually declined, losing one territory after another during the 19th century. These losses included Greece and Egypt; and at the conclusion of the 1914-18 war, Palestine, Syria and adjacent Arab territories which were also liberated from the Turk. What had been the eastern part of the Roman empire was eclipsed by the Turkish empire, and that in turn has now been reduced to a small republic occupying part of Asia Minor and the city of Istanbul on the European side of the Bosphorus.

Over the centuries, the national identities of the powers in control of an area changes, but the territories remain. Therefore in prophetic Scripture, we find nations referred to by the names by which they were originally known to the prophets and people of that time. This fact has led to the formula laid down by John Thomas, that the interpretation must be guided by "powers on territories". Thus, as we find the kings of the north and south returning to the scene in "the time of the end", the nations concerned will be different (except for the Jews), but must be identified by their control of the original territories.

From the point of view of the present, therefore, we have to keep in mind the territory occupied by the kings of south and north in the past. Present day Turkey in Asia Minor was part of the Seleucid kingdom, if not Byzantium (Istanbul) in Europe; but so, of course, was Lebanon, Syria, Iraq and Iran. A latter-day power, to qualify as "King of the North" should occupy all these territories, so we must anticipate some major changes in the map before the last few verses of chapter 11 can be fulfilled.

With the advent of the "abomination" and the consequent "desolation", the kings of the south and the north disappeared from the vision. The "king" fills the vacuum.

Therefore the reappearance of the kings of the south and the north at the end of chapter 11 (verse 40), presupposes a situation similar to that which existed before the desolation, that is, the return of a sizeable Jewish population to the land as aforetime; a situation which the Turks, following the Romans, had long prevented. This accounts for the long hiatus, during which few Jews were in the land, and little change took place that was *relevant to the scope of the vision* (see chapter 11, Appendix II).

Thus the kings of the south and the north cannot represent the Saracen/Turkish epoch. This is another example of premature anticipation in interpretation. Another point against the Saracens being the king of the south, and their successors the Turks being the king of the north, is that neither of them was distinctively either north or south, but overflowed *both* areas. In fact the Saracens invaded the north of Palestine *before* they invaded Egypt to the south.

The Kings of the South and North at the Time of the End

Verse 40: "And at the time of the end shall the king of the south push at him: and the king of the north shall come against him like a whirlwind, with chariots, and with horsemen, and with many ships; and he shall enter into the countries, and shall overflow and pass over.'' This king of the south used to be associated with Britain, because for some years Britain exercised a protectorate over Egypt; but Britain has retired from that responsibility since the 1914-18 war, and Egypt is now independent. Similarly, when we take a look at present trends, it seems inevitable that sooner or later Russia will fill the rôle of king of the north.

Whatever verse 40 means, it is to happen at ''the time of the end''. It may not be possible to place time limits on this expression, but in its several occurrences in Daniel 8 and the vision under review, it is used in close proximity with references to the resurrection of the dead, and the end of the age of Gentile rule, when God's kingdom will be ushered in. Daniel 8:17-19 associates similar words both before and after the symbolic resurrection of Daniel, and in chapter 12 the phrase is used in the same connection, in verses 4 and 9, just after the prophecy of the resurrection from the dead. We are therefore at a point in the vision where there is a rather indeterminate line between present and future.

It has been debated whether verse 40 means that the kings of the north and south resume attacking one another, or whether there is one (''him'') in between, who is the relic of the Roman ''king'', and who is ''pushed at'' successively by the kings of the south and the north, and thus finally removed from the map.[4]

As verse 40 is to occur at ''the time of the end'', we should now be able to arrive at an understanding of it. The erstwhile Turkish empire was a temporary representative on the territory of the Roman horn-cum-beast in the east, and the ''king of the south'' pushed at ''him'' from Egypt during World War I and cast him out of God's land. This had the result that the Turkish power collapsed, and Israel was enabled to form a National Home there with British and United Nations support.[5] It seems to remain for the ''king of the north'' to ''come against

---

4. This matter is discussed in *The Christadelphian*, 1918, p. 406; the argument turns on whether the ''king'' of verses 36-39 is regarded as ''the king of the north'' or as the ''little horn'' referred to in Daniel 8:9,22-23, a separate but temporary entity. *The Christadelphian*, 1942, pp.70,124 may also be relevant.

5. This interpretation concerns a ''king of the south'' restricted to a power occupying Egypt, and not like the Saracens occupying the territory of the north as well. In fact the first Saracens invaded the north before they invaded Egypt.

him" and to "overflow and pass over", that is, to engulf Constantinople and Turkey, and then to "enter the glorious land". However that may be, the overall picture is of the same basic theme as the other visions: the development of a human power which exalts itself and comes to an end in a time of trouble such as never was; at which time many rise from the dead to everlasting life.

The Final Conflict

Verses 41-45: "He shall enter also into the glorious land, and many countries shall be overthrown: but these shall escape out of his hand, even Edom, and Moab, and the chief of the children of Ammon. He shall stretch forth his hand also upon the countries: and the land of Egypt shall not escape. But he shall have power over the treasures of gold and of silver, and over all the precious things of Egypt: and the Libyans and the Ethiopians shall be at his steps. But tidings out of the east and out of the north shall trouble him: therefore he shall go forth with great fury to destroy, and utterly to make away many. And he shall plant the tabernacles of his palace between the seas in the glorious holy mountain; yet he shall come to his end, and none shall help him."

It is evident from verse 42 that Egypt, hitherto called "king of the south", falls before the king of the north and that Libya and Ethiopia will support him in a conflict still in the future. Edom, Moab and Ammon escape his clutches. This area is at present the kingdom of Jordan. The reason for their escape will no doubt become apparent when the time comes. Other prophecies regarding these nations use the phrase so often applied to Israel, that God will "bring again their captivity" in the latter days, except that Edom seems to be doomed to perpetual desolations (Jeremiah 49:13). But even there perhaps temporary space may be found for refugees. Elam (Persia, Iran) is the only other Gentile nation mentioned as being brought back from captivity in the latter days (see Jeremiah 48:47; 49:6,39).

What the tidings out of the east and north are to be remains to be seen, but it is certain that this latter day king of the north will invade the Holy Land, make his headquarters there, and be divinely destroyed for his temerity.

There have, of course, been seemingly cogent interpretations that verses 40-45 have already been fulfilled; there have been a number of "pushes" from the south (e.g. Mehemet Ali), taking place over the years, that have kept watchmen on their toes. It is considered that the

1917 "push" from the south that ejected the Turks from Palestine has had such world-shaking consequences, as to justify the interpretation here presented. In any case, Turkey has hardly yet been eliminated, and Egypt, Libya and Ethiopia are *still with us*, ready to be at the disposal of a future king of the north.

The re-appearance of the kings of the north and south at the end of this chapter requires the situation in the last days to be analogous to the times described earlier in the chapter.

CHAPTER 11: APPENDIX I

"The abomination that maketh desolate"

An "abomination" in the Biblical sense is an idol. The expression stems from Moses' description of Israel's experiences in the land of Moab before they crossed the Jordan river. Moses reminds them "how we came through the nations which ye passed by; and ye have seen their abominations, and their idols, wood and stone". And this was accompanied with the warning, "lest there should be among you man, or woman . . . whose heart turneth away this day from the Lord our God" (Deuteronomy 29:17-18).

Israel received strict injunctions not to imitate these nations: "Ye shall make you no idols nor graven image, neither rear you up a standing image . . .". And the penalty for not hearkening to God in this matter, "and if ye walk contrary unto me", was: "And I will make your cities waste, and bring your sanctuaries unto desolation . . . and I will bring the land into desolation . . . and your land shall be desolate and your cities waste" (Leviticus 26:1,21,31). Thus the "abomination" was the idol, and the "desolation" was the punishment for apostasy. The idol power, used to chastise Israel when they were unfaithful, was therefore, "the abomination of desolation".

There are several points of view regarding the interpretation of verses 30-31 of Daniel 11. One applies it to the desecration of the Temple by Antiochus Epiphanes, and the succeeding verses to the exploits of the Maccabees. A second view applies it to the desecration of the Temple by the Romans in A.D. 70, in which case the succeeding context applies to the experiences of the early Christians. A third view applies it to the Moslem "abomination" of which more anon.

The key to the interpretation surely lies in the words of Jesus in his Mount Olivet discourse. Matthew's record (24:15-16) reads, "When ye therefore shall see the abomination of desolation, spoken of by Daniel the prophet, stand in the holy place, (whoso readeth, let him understand:) then let them which be in Judea flee into the mountains." The record of Mark (13:14) reads, "But when ye shall see the abomination of desolation, spoken of by Daniel the Prophet, standing where it ought not, (let him that readeth understand,) then let them that be in Judea flee to the mountains." Luke simply says, "When ye shall see Jerusalem compassed with armies, then know that the desolation thereof is nigh. Then let them which are in Judea flee to the mountains . . . For these be the days of vengeance, that all things that are written may be fulfilled" (Luke 21:20-22).

It is well known from the writings of Josephus and other sources that the "abomination" the disciples of Jesus *saw*, and to the warning of which they responded, was the Roman one under Titus, when Roman legionaries sacrificed to their ensigns inside the Temple walls. The invasion of the Roman armies 40 years after the earthly mission of Jesus was completed was sufficient intimation to believers, not only to flee the city of Jerusalem, but also the province of Judea.

The words of Josephus are: "And now the Romans, upon the flight of the seditious into the city, and upon the burning of the holy house itself, and of all the buildings round about it, brought their ensigns to the temple, and set them over against its eastern gate; and there did they offer sacrifices to them, and there did they make Titus imperator, with the greatest acclamations of joy. And now all the soldiers had such vast quantities of spoils which they had gotten by plunder, that in Syria a pound weight of gold was sold for half its former value" (*Wars*, chapter VI, para. 1). A footnote attributes to Tertullian the following: "The entire religion of the Roman camp almost consisted in worshipping the ensigns, in swearing by the ensigns, and in preferring the ensigns before all (other) gods."

In the prophecy of Daniel we encounter three occasions where expressions similar to the quotation of Jesus occur. We have to determine whether the words of Jesus link the three together as all referring to the same incident, or whether Jesus is only alluding specifically to one of them. We have already reviewed the first of them in Daniel 9:27: "And he shall confirm the covenant with many for one week: and in the midst of the week he shall cause the sacrifice and the oblation to cease, and *for the overspreading of abominations he shall make it desolate*, even until the consummation, and that determined, shall be poured upon the desolator" (margin). Modern translations vary the phraseology, but do not seem to add much intelligibility.

The situation of this verse in the context of chapter 9, after the completion of the 70th week which included the cutting off of the Messiah, involves that it cannot apply to the time of Antiochus Epiphanes, but may be what Jesus was referring to. The disciples did see the Roman introduction of the abomination, but not the later Moslem one, which the use of the plural "abominations" may be thought to include, but it could also include Jewish abominations.

The second reference is Daniel 11:31: "And arms shall stand on his part, and they shall pollute the sanctuary of strength, and shall take away the daily sacrifice, and they shall place the abomination that maketh desolate. And such as do wickedly against the covenant shall he corrupt by flatteries . . ." On the score that the Romans have entered the arena in the guise of "ships of Chittim", and that the narrator alters his pronoun to "they" in reference to them, it is interpreted by some that it is *they*—the Romans—that do the polluting and placing of the abomination that maketh desolate, and therefore the passage is applied to the episode of A.D. 70. This leaves a hiatus in the middle of the narrative of the war between the kings of the north and south. Antiochus Epiphanes is left in suspended animation as it were, with no particularly appropriate application of the phrase following, "And such as do wickedly against the covenant shall he corrupt by flatteries"—if Antiochus Epiphanes is the "he" of this phrase.

The phrase, "And arms shall stand on his part," whilst superficially appearing to be acting for Antiochus Epiphanes against the Jews, could be interpreted as being Roman arms acting with the same motives as those of Antiochus Epiphanes, at a later date; this would allow for the conflation suggested in the text of our exposition. In verse 31, Young's Literal Translation reads, "And strong ones out of him stand up," whilst the LXX reads, "And seeds spring up out of him"—conveying the idea that it is a later generation that perpetrates the profanation of the Sanctuary.

The third reference to "the abomination that maketh desolate" is in Daniel 12:11: "And from the time that the daily sacrifice shall be taken away, and the abomination that maketh desolate set up, there shall be a thousand two hundred and ninety days." The phrase "taken away" is rendered in N.I.V. "abolished", and in Berkeley "eliminated". Taken in this sense the passage cannot be applied to Antiochus Epiphanes, because in that instance the sacrifices were not abolished, only suspended for three years.

In view of the general theme of the vision to define the "indignation" of God at the behaviour of mankind relative to his Messiah, His Anointed Saviour Son, we conclude that all the prophecies relative to the abomination of desolation refer primarily to the *complete suspension* of the evening-morning oblation and other rituals of the Law, which occurred in A.D. 70. The temporary suspension in 168 B.C., was only a *portent*. Jesus perceived this clearly.

In the third reference, however, some apply the "abomination" to the Moslem mosques built on Mount Moriah at a much later date. This is based partly on the words of a Catholic prelate, and partly on the interpretation of the time period in the same verse, which will be considered in due course.

CHAPTER 11: APPENDIX II

The Jews of Palestine, A.D. 70—1917

Cestius Gallus started the siege of Jerusalem in A.D. 66, but inexplicably withdrew, giving the Christians the opportunity to flee to Pella. The Emperor Nero called in Vespasian and his son Titus to renew the attack; in 69 Vespasian was proclaimed Emperor, and in the capturing of Jerusalem by Titus in A.D. 70 over 1 million Jews perished and 95,000 were exported as slaves or used as victims in the Roman games.

A few years later, in A.D. 130, the Emperor Hadrian decided to build Aelia Capitolina on the site of Jerusalem. This precipitated the revolt of a pseudo-messiah Bar-Cochba. Ruthless suppression of this rebellion decimated the population of Judea in A.D. 135. More than half-a-million men were killed, nearly 1,000 villages destroyed and in Judea Jews were virtually exterminated, and none allowed within sight of Jerusalem. This exclusion from Jerusalem was known as the Edict of Hadrian. It was not officially withdrawn until 1856, when the Sultan of Turkey suddenly changed his policy and proclaimed the land no longer closed to Jews.

The centre of surviving Jewish life moved to Galilee, and Tiberias became their most important centre of learning (ca. 199-279); but owing to further ravages of revolts and war, this gradually declined. There had been a trickle of immigrants from Babylon at this time. Consequent upon the establishment of Christianity as the religion of the Roman Empire in 323, the "moral and physical pressure on the Jews hastened the process, and at the beginning of the 5th century the Patriarchate, already in decline, was finally abolished by the Roman authorities" (A.D. 425).

Immigration ended for the next few centuries. Jerusalem fell to the Arabs in 638. Abd-al-Malik (685-705) is credited with the erection of "The Dome of the Rock" (691), when both Christian and Jewish pilgrims were tolerated. In the subsequent period Palestine was often reduced to a battlefield between Christians and Arabs. From 996-1021, the Moslems reactivated the discriminatory laws which had previously been imposed on Christians and Jews. It is claimed that ca. 1170 there were 1,000 Jewish families in Palestine.

Immigration ceased during the Crusader-Moslem battles. In 1187 Saladin expelled the Christians, but allowed Jews into Jerusalem again. The Turks later massacred Christians and killed some Jews as well. Immigration was resumed in the 14th and 15th centuries owing to pressures in outside countries. The Turkish conquest took place in 1516; there are said to have been 14,000 Jews in the Land in 1567. In the 17th century, Safed became the most important centre for Jews drifting in from Europe, but in 1714 1,500 arrived and were dispersed by various misfortunes. It is claimed there were, in 1741, 10,000 Jews in Jerusalem called "Hasidim".

Yet according to the private diary of Sir Moses Montefiore, he could find no more than 500 Jews, existing in the poorest circumstances, when he toured the land in 1827. He obtained a firman from the Porte to build 27 cottages outside the south-west walls of Jerusalem in 1838, but it was not until 1856 that their erection was finally accomplished. In relating this in his book *Palestine and the Jews*, F. G. Jannaway also lists 58 Jewish colonies which had been established between 1852 and 1910.

In 1835 Jews were permitted to repair their four synagogues, and gradually attained "freedom of religion" for the first time in hundreds of years. In 1850 Jews were drifting in, mostly on the basis of religious sentiment. In 1865 Jews in Jerusalem were in the majority for the first time in 1800 years. In 1900 there were 28,200 Jews out of a population of 45,600.

After the French withdrawal (Napoleon, 1801), Egypt came under the rule of the Viceroy Mohammed Ali, who occupied Palestine in 1831, and under him and his son Ibrahim the Holy Land enjoyed "a fairly enlightened administration. Their tolerant rule opened the country to western influence." The Powers, however, supported the Sultan, but induced him to introduce "reforms", which later resulted in a marked increase in the inflow of foreign settlements and colonies from Europe, most important of which were Zionist agricultural settlements (1882).

In 1887 Robert Roberts had contacts with Laurence Oliphant who lived on Mt. Carmel, and was interested in the development of the Holy Land. In *The Christadelphian*, 1887, p. 36, he records a conversation with him of which the following are short extracts: "The land had splendid resources which only required security for their development. They could not be developed under Turkish law, which meant uncertainty, delay, obstruction and perpetual backsheesh ..." Oliphant "was the only resident Englishman in the country holding land, and the only man who knew the ways of the country. Nothing could be done on an extensive scale while Turkish authority existed in the country. It was not merely that the laws were lax and dilatory; but a systematic policy of obstruction was observed in reference to everything in the way of improvement. The Turkish Government entertained an extreme jealousy of everything bringing influence into the country or likely to lead to nationality. The authorities would confirm no sale, and enforce no mortgage, to a stranger. A stranger might lend his money, but natives were not allowed to give security. Even money as a present was not accepted from strangers . . .''

Later in the year Viccars Collyer visited the Holy Land and contacted Oliphant. In a letter to Robert Roberts he writes (pp. 327-8 of the same Magazine): ''There are more Jews *now* in Palestine than is generally supposed. Statistics regarding them are not reliable, and it is not in their interest that it should be known how their numbers increase. The Turkish Government is striving *all it can* to prevent them coming to the Holy Land, but they do come, most of them perhaps ostensibly as pilgrims. Jews are not allowed to purchase land, but still there are Jews who *own* land, and their numbers are increasing. 'Christians' can purchase land, but the government do not like it, and to prevent the sale of land to 'Christians', have sometimes imprisoned those who have sold land to them. This block of the Turk is not without its advantages, as apart from it, Palestine would have been full of Gentiles long before this.''

1896 saw the publication of *Der Judenstaat* (The Jewish State) by Theodor Herzl, and the colonies subsidized by Baron Edmond de Rothschild rose from 22 in 1900 to 47 in 1918. Most Jews were town-dwellers. The population of Palestine in 1914 was 690,000 of which 535,000 were Moslem, 70,000 Christian, and 85,000 Jews. The Balfour Declaration of 1917 saw the beginning of Jewish immigration on a big scale.

As suggested in our exposition of chapter 11, the kings of the south and north are active before, and at the end of this period when the Jews could freely practise their religion as they wished. In between, being numerically very few, the Jews were in a state of religious repression, during the absence of these ''kings'' from the vision. Therefore the kings of the south and north do not represent Saracens and Turks.

Sources: *Encyclopaedia Britannica; Immigration & Settlement* (Israel Pocket Library); *The Christadelphian* Magazine, 1887; F. G. Jannaway, *Palestine and the Jews*, 1914.

CHAPTER 12

DANIEL's Third Vision now comes to its conclusion: "And at that time shall Michael stand up, the great prince which standeth for the children of thy people: and there shall be a time of trouble, such as never was since there was a nation even to that same time: and at that time thy people shall be delivered, every one that shall be found written in the book. And many of them that sleep in the dust of the earth shall awake, some to everlasting life, and some to shame and everlasting contempt'' (12:1-2).

"The time of the end"

We believe we are now well into the "time of the end", and expectant of Michael standing up. In considering the beginning of this vision, we asked "Who is Michael?" He is the great prince who stands for the people of Daniel, the Jews. However, because the context takes us through the resurrection from the dead, the statement in Hebrews 2:5 becomes relevant: "Unto the angels hath he not put in subjection the world to come, whereof we speak." In other words, Jesus, having been crowned with glory and honour, will be the ruler in the "world to come", which is the kingdom of God, so that it will no longer be in subjection to angels. Therefore, in this verse "Michael" is taken by John Thomas to be a title of Jesus. It is difficult to see how the same name can apply to two different parties in the same vision (compare 10:13,21 with 12:1).

Until the institution of the Kingdom, there is clearly work for the angelic Michael to do, even though Peter's reference to the authority of Jesus is also relevant. Peter says of Jesus Christ, that he is "gone into heaven, and is on the right hand of God; angels and authorities and powers being made subject unto him".

When Jesus returns in power and great glory, to take unto himself his great power and to reign, it will also be the time for the kingdoms to be taken away from human national governments, and to be given to the "saints of the most High" who will possess the Kingdom. No doubt as Michael "stands up" on behalf of Jewry prior to the take-over of power during the "time of trouble", the situation will arise in which it will be appropriate for him to hand over his responsibilities to Jesus. In this sense, perhaps the title may play a dual role: for Jesus is *literally* the "One like God".

There is coming upon the earth a time of unparallelled trouble and distress. Politicians are even now struggling to avoid the consequences of the "arms race" which their fears and jealousies have led them into for so long. The *possibilities* are hundreds of times more dreadful than Hiroshima and Nagasaki. Did not Jesus speak of "distress of nations with perplexity", of "no way out", of "men's hearts failing them for fear, and for looking after those things which are coming on the earth" (Luke 21:25-26), just before they see him "coming in a cloud with power and great glory"? In his Revelation Jesus speaks of destroying "them which destroy the earth"; and of "the cities of the nations" falling, in connection with his return to rule the earth (Revelation 11:18; 16:19). In the context this trouble is coincident with the resurrection from the dead, and those whose "names are written in the book", or as Jesus puts it in Luke 10:20, "written in heaven", will be delivered from it.

The Resurrection

Jesus takes up the words of the narrating angel (verse 2), and asserts the authority God has accorded to him, "As the Father raiseth up the dead, and quickeneth them; even so the Son quickeneth whom he will. For the Father judgeth no man, but hath committed all judgement unto the Son: that all men should honour the Son, even as they honour the Father". They who hear and believe the Son, stand related to everlasting life; and "the hour is coming, in the which all that are in the graves shall hear his voice (remember how Daniel heard the 'Man' whilst he lay asleep?), and shall come forth; they that have done good, unto the resurrection of life; and they that have done evil, unto the resurrection of condemnation" (John 5:21-29).

The same epoch that sees the resurrection from the dead, sees also the restoration of the Jewish nation. By analogy, this is spoken of as a resurrection also. Daniel's contemporary prophet, Ezekiel, prophesied about the "valley of dry bones": "Thus saith the Lord God; Behold, O my people, I will open your graves, and cause you to come up out of your graves, and bring you into the land of Israel. And ye shall know that I am the LORD, when I have opened your graves, O my people, and brought you up out of your graves, and shall put my spirit

THE PROPHECY OF DANIEL

in you, and ye shall live, and I shall place you in your own land: then
shall ye know that I the LORD have spoken it, and performed it, saith
the LORD'' (37:12-14).

Again, in a context dealing with the restoration of Israel, Hosea says
on behalf of God: "I will ransom them from the power of the grave;
I will redeem them from death: O death, I will be thy plagues; O grave,
I will be thy destruction: repentance shall be hid from mine eyes"
(13:14). These words are appropriated by Paul to apply to the literal
resurrection: "So when this corruptible shall have put on incorruption,
and this mortal shall have put on immortality, then shall be brought to
pass the saying that is written, Death is swallowed up in victory. O
death, where is thy sting? O grave, where is thy victory? ... Thanks
be to God, which giveth us the victory through our Lord Jesus Christ"
(1 Corinthians 15:54-57).

We are therefore led to conclude that the return of Israel to their land,
which we have watched taking place in recent decades, is a certain
indication that we are in "the time of the end" (verse 4), and a sure
portent of the imminence of the literal resurrection from the dead, and
of the return of the Master. "Watch ye therefore, and pray always, that
ye may be accounted worthy to escape all these things that shall come
to pass, and to stand before the Son of man" (Luke 21:36). Yet, "we
which are alive and remain unto the coming of the Lord shall not
prevent (lit. precede) them that are asleep" (1 Thessalonians 4:15).

What Daniel is told is very succinct. Michael is said to "stand up ...
for the children of thy people", who would appear to be the Jews. Then
there is a reference to "a time of trouble, such as never was". Next,
"at that time thy people shall be delivered, every one that shall be found
written in the book". One would interpret this phrase "thy people" as
meaning the saints of whom those who are found in the book are
delivered either from the trouble, or from death. Inasmuch as two
phrases cannot be uttered simultaneously, it is recorded immediately
that many that are asleep in the dust will awake, some to everlasting
life. It would appear that in the world-wide confusion and distress of
this time of trouble, the resurrection could pass unnoticed by "the man
in the street".

The several phrases of verse 1 could well be contemporary or over-
lapping. The judgement seat is not mentioned in so many words; but
it is implied by the phrase "some to everlasting life, and some to shame
and everlasting contempt", and also by the clause "thy people ...

140

found written in the book". If this is not to be understood to mean "the book of life", it must be restricted to deliverance of the living from "the time of trouble" only—a privilege which would only be meaningful if it was followed by justification at the judgement. Nor should the application of this passage be restricted to the Jews, because "the saints" which we know includes all the redeemed, ancient and modern, Jew and Gentile, have already been mentioned several times in Daniel's dream of chapter 7.

As a result of the resurrection and judgement, "They that be wise shall shine as the brightness of the firmament; and they that turn many to righteousness as the stars for ever and ever" (verse 3). In one of his parables Jesus says, "Then shall the righteous shine forth as the sun in the kingdom of their Father" (Matthew 13:43).

Turning many to righteousness is no passive rôle. It is a double-edged activity. It is not only advantageous to those who respond, but it demonstrates our own commitment to Christ. It is, in fact, part of a warfare. A few Scriptures come to mind:

"Earnestly contend for the faith which was once delivered unto the saints" (Jude 3).

"He which converteth the sinner from the error of his way shall save a soul from death, and shall hide a multitude of sins" (James 5:20).

"The weapons of our warfare are not carnal, but mighty through God to the pulling down of strongholds; casting down imaginations, and every high thing that exalteth itself against the knowledge of God, and bringing into captivity every thought to the obedience of Christ" (2 Corinthians 10:4,5).

"The fruit of the righteous is a tree of life; and he that winneth souls is wise" (Proverbs 11:30).

"The path of the just is as the shining light, that shineth more and more unto the perfect day" (Proverbs 4:18).

Running to and fro

With this picture of the destiny of the righteous, the subject changes. Daniel is told to "shut up the words, and seal the book, even to the time of the end: many shall run to and fro, and knowledge shall be increased" (verse 4). The inference seems to be that at "the time of the end", the meaning of the vision would be understood. Therefore many interpret the running to and fro to be in Bible study, and that it is *Scriptural* knowledge that will be increased. The advice given is, however, just the opposite to that given to Habakkuk: "The Lord answered me and said, Write the vision, and make it plain upon tables, that he may run that readeth it. For the vision is yet for an appointed time, but at the end it shall speak, and not lie: though it tarry, wait for it; because it will surely come, it will not tarry" (2:2). It is possible to read "run" to mean 'direct one's life accordingly'; or alternatively, 'to seek a place of safety in a city of refuge'.

But, the Hebrew word for "run" in this passage is different from the one used in Daniel 12:4. That word is rather uncommon, and in several instances has a very general meaning of moving about for various purposes. Two instances speak of the "eyes of the Lord" running to and fro through the earth (2 Chronicles 16:9; Zechariah 4:10); Jeremiah, using the same metaphor, speaks of *seeking* a righteous man because of his rarity in Jerusalem (5:1); and Amos uses the word in regard to seeking for "the word of the Lord" and not finding it (8:12), rather than of understanding it when it is in one's possession.

The difficulty with the above interpretation lies in the word "many". The number of people in these "latter days", who even partially understand the vision seems deplorably *few* when compared with the world's population, or even if we restrict the comparison to professing Christians. Even with those few who comprehend a broad outline of the prophecy, the studiousness implied by the "running to and fro" is less marked than we would like to see it.

The Berkeley Bible's rendering of the verse is as follows: "But you Daniel, keep the message a secret; seal the book until the final period; many shall investigate and information shall advance". The N.I.V. reads, "Many will go here and there to increase knowledge". If therefore we give the phrases of the A.V. a simple superficial interpretation, and regard them as general characteristics of the "time of the end", they are transformed into a "sign of the times" which has developed out of all proportion. "Knowledge" in the technical sense outstrips men's ability to put it into service—and how they travel!

How long?

The scene now changes back to the great river Hiddekel. The symbolic Man of the Spirit is above the water, and angels stand on either bank. The symbolic Man is asked a question: "How long shall it be to the end of these wonders?" (verse 6). Daniel observes that in reply, the Man "held up his right hand and his left hand unto heaven, and sware by him that liveth for ever that it shall be for a time, times, and a half; and when he shall have accomplished to scatter the power of the holy people, all these things shall be finished" (verse 7). Once again, Daniel confesses, "I heard, but I understood not", and enquires, "O my Lord, what shall be the end of these things?" (verse 8). From a symbolic Man, he received a symbolic answer.

Yet again we have something hidden from his generation; it seems evident that it would not become "understood" until events made it fairly obvious. In the vision the "man clothed in linen ... sware by him that liveth for ever". Clearly this represents something very important indeed, and the action reminds us of the fact that God *confirmed* His covenants by an *oath*. "It shall be for a time, times and a half; and when he shall have accomplished to scatter the power of the holy people, all these things shall be finished".

The obscurity of the answer shows that it is enigmatical and symbolic, as previously noted in other cases. The form of words, and its indefinite application, seem like a reminder—a reiteration of the former pronouncement made in chapter 7:25-26, where it is said of the "little horn" on the head of the fourth (Roman) beast, "He shall speak great words against the most High, and shall wear out the saints of the most High, and think to change times and laws: and they shall be given into his hand until a time and times and the dividing of time. But the judgement shall sit, and they shall take away his dominion, to consume and to destroy it unto the end". God has "confirmed" this promise with an oath.

The "time, times and a half" (just half the seven times considered in chapter 4), is equivalent to 1260 day-years on the principles already discussed (see Chapter 4: Appendix I, page 41). A second period of 1290, and a third of 1335 are also given. Earlier expositors regarded these time periods as having a *common ending*, which would culminate in Daniel's standing in his "lot", or in other words the establishment of the Kingdom of God. As expected at the time, this ending was marked by the fall of the temporal power of the Papacy; and it was also anticipated that the next event, speedily to follow, would be the appearance of the Master and the establishment of the Kingdom.

It soon became obvious that this joint-ending application was erroneous. It was next suggested that only the 1260-day period ended with this "fall", and that the periods would have a common *starting point*. This meant that the second period would overlap the fall of the temporal power by 30 years, and the third by a further 45 years. Time has since disproved this interpretation also, at least in respect of the 1335 period. We must therefore view each period separately.

In interpreting this prophecy, expositors have shown that from the time when the Papacy gained its acknowledged primacy, commonly called "the decree of Phocas", about A.D. 607-610, to its loss of temporal power in A.D. 1867-1870 when the French took over the administration of the Papal States, was a period of 1260 years.

Since that time the power of the Papacy to persecute the saints has been broken. The decree of Phocas is supposed to have conceded to the Roman Bishop spiritual primacy in all countries, with jurisdiction over all churches of east and west. Even if we do not regard the historicity of this "decree" as sufficiently supported, the fact remains that Pope Gregory the Great commenced a new phase in Papal development. He became Pope in A.D. 590, and is said to have stated that such a title as Universal Bishop and Supreme Head of the Church was a badge of the precursor of Antichrist.

Yet within a few years, in A.D. 606, Pope Boniface III apparently adopted the title. The authorities for its bestowal upon him by "the decree of Phocas" are Anastasius and Paulus Diaconus, who lived in the 9th and 8th centuries respectively; so they could have had no interest in the application of the "time, times and a half" or 1260 days.

We may also take note that a date thirty years after the fall of the temporal power saw the first Zionist Congress in Basle A.D. 1897, which gave such an impetus to the idea of a national home for the Jews, and has led to their regathering to Israel. The sign given in the next phrase in Daniel 12 is, "when he shall have accomplished to scatter the power of the holy people, all these things shall be finished". The period of "a time, times and a half", does not include the Zionist movement: it precedes it; and the phrase "accomplished to scatter" (which seems rather ambiguous in the A.V.), is usually rendered in modern versions in the sense that the 1290 days mark the end and reversal of the scattering of the Jews, as the previous period had marked the end of the suppression of the saints.

The "idea" materialized in the promulgation of the Balfour Declaration, one outcome of World War I, that the British Government favoured the establishment of a National Home for the Jews, in the land of Palestine.

Rome is the subject of the judgements of this vision. Rome suppressed the Mosaic institution in Judea, and eventually became the Christianized "mother of harlots and abominations" which achieved its maturity, or was "set up", in A.D. 607-610, and is due for the ultimate destruction of which 1870 was a portent. The Papal supremacy was achieved in stages; its fall likewise is coming in stages, commencing from the time of the French Revolution. The phenomenon of a more popular and apparently more tolerant Roman Church which we see at the present time is a *revival*. "I sit a queen and am no widow", is a stage in Papal development signified in the book of Revelation, but which is not clearly indicated by Daniel.

We can therefore conclude that the starting point for the period of 1290 day-years is the same as for the time, times and a half. The sign which ended the one, by inference constitutes the commencement of the overlap of the other, opening the way for the regathering of the Jews, whereby the time of the scattering of their power will be "accomplished" or "finished" (verse 7).

The 1335 days has no defined beginning, and only a vague ending sign, associated with a time of blessing; and, inferentially, of Daniel's rising from his rest and standing in his "lot". As we are without a starting point, we must await developments to clarify the application.

The prophecies are not given to enable *us* to prophesy the future, but to provide us with grounds for comfort and confidence as we see the forecasts coming to fruition, often in totally unexpected ways.

We cannot afford to neglect this source of spiritual strength. Current materialism constantly tends to draw our minds away from the Spirit's ideas; we must therefore cultivate the mind of the Messiah, who *pointed us to Daniel*. He is the Anointed One whose cause we have espoused. We have participated in his "shame" and have "taken up the cross"; we may therefore share his glory. Let us then follow his gaze—"Let him that readeth understand" Daniel the prophet!

"Seal the book"

To gather up the remaining verses for brief comment: in verse 4, Daniel is told to "shut up the words and seal the book, even to the time of the end". Evidently it was not intended to be understood until that time. He had been told the same thing in chapter 8:26, and so Daniel's enquiries are cut short with the words, "Go thy way, Daniel: for the words *are* closed up and sealed till the time of the end". The word "closed" is the same in Hebrew as "shut" in verse 4. This compares with the Apocalyptic sealing of what the thunderous voices uttered, but contrasts with the final revelation which Jesus conveyed to John (Revelation 22:10): "Seal not the sayings of the prophecy of this book: for the time is at hand". The succeeding idea in Revelation 22 is also very similar to that in Daniel 12: "Many shall be purified, and made white, and tried; but the wicked shall do wickedly: and none of the wicked shall understand; but the wise shall understand".

If we are purified by the word, and respond faithfully to our tribulations, we shall be blessed with Daniel by standing in our "lot" at the end of the days. "Blessed is he that waiteth." The impact of this final chapter is upon both Jews and saints. Chapter 12 has brought us to the last event revealed in the vision. It is the event to which all the visions lead; their consummation is the establishment of the Kingdom of God. The resurrection of the "saints" and their glorification is the necessary prelude, but what the Kingdom will be like Daniel is not told. He knew that what was represented by the fourth beast, the metallic image, and the king of fierce countenance, would be destroyed and disappear without trace. He knew that the sanctuary would be cleansed, and that he would stand in his lot at the end of the days; and that when this happened, like his as yet unborn Master, he would see the travail of his soul and be satisfied.

Near the end of the days, as we are, let us continue the study of this prophecy and the New Testament ones that unlock it, with bright spiritual eyes and sharpened vision to detect what little remains to be fulfilled before the great trumpet blast calls us to stand with Daniel before the Son of man. Daniel's visions were granted as a result of his concern about the expiry of the seven decades of Jewish captivity. His prayer contributed directly to at least two of them. We are on the threshold of the expiry of *seven times* from that epoch; what is our prayer?

"O Lord, according to all thy righteousness, I beseech thee, let thine anger and thy fury be turned away from thy city Jerusalem, thy holy mountain: because for our sins, and for the iniquities of our fathers, Jerusalem and thy people are become a reproach to all that are about us. Now therefore, O our God, hear the prayer of thy servant, and his supplications, and cause thy face to shine upon thy sanctuary that is desolate, for the Lord's sake. O my God, incline thine ear, and hear ... O Lord, forgive; O Lord, hearken and do" (9:16-19).

Jesus foresaw an army lay siege to Jerusalem and an "abomination" stand in the Holy Place. He advised believers witnessing the gathering forces, to flee the city. They went to Pella.

> "Who was saved when desolation
> Fell on Salem's guilty head?
> When th' accurs'd 'abomination'
> All 'the holy place' o'erspread?
> Friends of Jesus—
> They alone to Pella fled!"

We are on the threshold of similar events, and Jesus also has a message for us. "Spirits of devils ... go forth unto the kings of the earth and of the whole world, to gather them to the battle of that great day of God Almighty. Behold, I come as a thief. *Blessed is he that watcheth and keepeth his garments*, lest he walk naked, and they see his shame. And he gathered them together into a place called Armageddon".

In our case the path to safety is spiritual, not physical.

CHAPTER 12: APPENDIX I

The Time Periods and the Decree of Phocas

The sources given in the footnote[1] offer useful background. Guinness says Gregory "constitutes a very leading date in the rise of the Papacy", and quotes Archbishop Trench as saying that he was "the first of the Latin Fathers, and *the first in the modern sense of the word of the Popes*"; he "did more than any other to set the Church forward upon the new lines on which henceforth it must travel to constitute a Latin Christianity, with distinctive features of its own, such as broadly separate it from Greek" (R. C. Trench, *Mediaeval Church History*, p. 14, as quoted by Guinness).

Guinness (p. 612) also quotes Paulus Diaconus and Anastasius; and the Latin inscription on the Pillar of Phocas at Rome (table, p. 618). Faber makes the same points about the importance of the "Decree of Phocas" and after quoting Baronius in a footnote adds: "Some, I believe, have doubted whether such a grant was ever made by Phocas; but, as it appears to me, without much reason. We know how severely the title of Universal Bishop was reprobated by Pope Gregory at the end of the sixth, and at the beginning of the seventh century; we know likewise that the title was borne not long afterwards by the Roman Pontiff, and that it was formally confirmed to him by the Second Council of Nice in the year 787. Hence we are certain that it cannot have been assumed very late in the seventh century". He then refers to Anastasius and Paulus Diaconus, and contends that if the "decree" is a forgery, it was both unnecessary and most ill-contrived, since in A.D. 787 the Council of Nice had solemnly declared the Pope Universal Bishop. Papal defenders were too wily to choose such an infamous monster as Phocas for the purpose. Had it never been made by *any* Emperor, they would have chosen a more reputable patron.

---

1. H. Grattan Guinness, *The Approaching End of the Age*, pp. 375,379 (10th edition, 1886); J. Thomas, *Exposition of Daniel*, p. 109; *Eureka*, Vol. IIIa, pp. 232-237 (current edition); Faber, *A Dissertation on the Prophecies*, Vol. I.

CHAPTER 12: APPENDIX II

The Time Periods of Chapter 12: Moslem or Papal?

H. Grattan Guinness was a well-known exponent of the Moslem interpretation and Faber adopted a similar view in *The Sacred Calendar*. The basic idea is that the Roman Empire was divided into two in the fourth and fifth centuries, and each section developed a "little horn" which grew into a religious power manifested as an "abomination" in Jerusalem. After pagan Rome suppressed the "daily" sacrifices in A.D. 70, and a later Emperor, Constantine, retired from Rome to Constantinople, it was left to the Bishop of Rome to "set up" his Christianized "abomination" in the West. This "little horn" matured about 600 years after Christ, in the midst of ten Gothic kingdoms which had invaded and chastised the Western Catholics in the fifth to seventh centuries, but which eventually also adopted the Pope's religion.

Meanwhile in the East, the Catholic Emperor was also afflicted by an alternative "little horn" in the form of the Moslem Saracens and Turks who invaded the Eastern Empire at the very time the Pope's position was being consolidated.

Mohammed started his revelations and proclaimed himself a prophet in A.D. 610. He fled his persecuting fellow-tribesmen from Mecca to Medina in A.D. 622 from which date the Moslem Calendar commenced on a *lunar* basis. The Arabs captured Jerusalem in A.D. 637, whereupon the Greek Catholic Patriarch Sophronius privately commented that "the abomination of desolation" was now standing in the holy place, not appreciating that he was the representative of an "abomination" himself. The Arabs encompassed Syria in 636-638, Egypt in 640-642 and Mesopotamia in 639-646. They also spread along the coast of north Africa. In other words they occupied the territory of both the king of the south *and* most of the territory of the king of the north.

The power that had resided in the person of Mohammed, on his death was established in a Caliph, a sort of Moslem Pope with Imperial powers. All this time the Byzantine Empire was shrinking and getting weaker. By the 11th century, the Seljuks reinforced the Saracen

THE PROPHECY OF DANIEL

affliction and eventually, in A.D. 1453, their Turkish successors extinguished the Byzantine Empire. Are the Moslem invaders to be regarded as a "little horn" as Faber and Grattan Guinness and others argue, or as the chastisers of the erstwhile Roman "little horn"? As the little horn of the Goat which had emerged so much earlier had grown into the Roman Fourth Beast, it seems that the two "little horns" should not be placed in juxtaposition in this way.

Since 1453 the Mohammedan "abomination" has prevailed for about 400 years in the East until, in modern times, it has itself shrunk and been denuded of its many constituent parts. Though ejected from Palestine in 1917, it still, at the time of writing, lingers on in the Turkish republic in Asia Minor and Istanbul; Turkey used to be called "the sick man of Europe".

The question that has exercised the minds of many is: Are the time periods of Daniel 12 to be interpreted according to the Moslem abomination of 610/622/637 on a lunar scale, or according to the "setting up" of the Papal abomination 606/610 on a solar scale? The following table illustrates the alternatives:

A COMPARISON OF THE ARGUMENTS

Moslem	Papal
The worst desolator	The worst idolator = worst abomination
A scourge on Eastern "Christians"	A scourge on Saints
Abomination "set up" immediately; Mosque of Omar A.D. 637; Sophronius mutters "The abomination of desolation is in the holy place"	"Abomination" in Jerusalem in A.D. 70, but not "set up" till A.D. 606-610 in Rome—but cf. Zechariah 5:11, not to be rooted in Jerusalem
Moslem Times: Lunar* year 354 days	*Papal Times:* Solar* year 365 days
Mohammed's proclamation as Prophet A.D. 610; his flight from Mecca to Medina = Hegira A.D. 622; Capture of Jerusalem A.D. 637	

*1260 lunar = 1222½ solar
 1290 lunar = 1251½ solar
 1335 lunar = 1295 solar

150

Moslem (continued)

A.H.* 1260 $= 622 + 1222\frac{1}{2} =$
A.D. 1844

(a) Under constraint of Western powers, Turkey brought into operation "Tangimat", granting toleration to Christians

(b) Emergence of King of South, Mohammed Ali revolted in Egypt

(c) $622 + 1260$ solar $= 1882$; Britain in Egypt $=$ King of South

(d) $1844 = 391$ years 1 month after 1453 (Revelation 9:15) = beginning of deliverance of Jews = beginning of outpouring on Moslem desolator; therefore "setting up of desolator" undoubtedly A.D. 622

A.H. 1290 $=$ A.D. $622 + 1251\frac{1}{2} =$
A.D. 1873: during succeeding years marked by revolts of several more countries
$637 + 1251\frac{1}{2} = 1888\frac{1}{2}$;
$637 + 1290$ solar $= 1927$

A.H. 1335 $=$ A.D.
$622 + 1295 = 1917$
Balfour Declaration, Nov. 2;
Jerusalem delivered from Turk, Dec. 9; Turk calendar ended; change to solar calendar

JERUSALEM
Moslem abomination "set up" 622;
Jerusalem captured 637;
Turkey became "little horn of goat" 1453; removed from Palestine by Britain 1917 = 1335 lunar years from "setting up"

Papal (continued)

1260 $= 3\frac{1}{2}$ times $= 606\text{-}610$ to $1866\text{-}1870 =$ Decree of Phocas and dedication of Pantheon, to Fall of Temporal Power (Daniel 7:8,11, 20-22,25-26); confirmed by an oath (12:7) = freedom of saints from persecution

1290 $= 1260 + 30 =$ *A.D. 1897-1900*
1st Zionist Congress, Basle, 1897;
4th Zionist Congress, London, 1900:
Jewish aspirations

1335 $= 530\text{-}533$ to $1868 =$ Justinian to Fall of Temporal Power;
A.D. 610 to 1945, cessation World War II; paved way for surrender of Mandate and

State of Israel, 1948, but still no blessing of resurrection

---

*Anno Hegira

THE PROPHECY OF DANIEL

The Moslem expiry of the 1335 lunar years in 1917 is an interesting and significant pointer, but it is not the real thing. The "blessing" which is undoubtedly associated with resurrection, and therefore also with the Master's return, cannot be dated until after the event.

Taking an overall view of the book of Daniel alone, neither the metallic image nor the four beasts supply any symbolism of *Islam*. The Ram and Goat vision introduces a "little horn" growing out of one of the wings of the Greek empire, which "waxed exceeding great, toward the south, and *toward the east* and toward the pleasant land", but with no religious overtones except such as belong to the eastern Emperor's implied deification and his relationship with the Papacy in Rome. So far as *symbolism* is concerned we have not encountered Islam throughout the book. The argument is that the Moslems were God's Unitarian avenging agency upon Eastern Christendom, just as the Goths were a scourge in the West. The more detailed symbolism belongs to the Apocalypse.

The debatable points of view can be read in *The Christadelphian* for 1892, p. 292; 1893, p. 450; 1904, p. 436; 1927, p. 23; 1957, p. 379, 412, 425; and other sources, old and new. There is quite an element of "premature anticipation" in these articles, but perhaps that shows that the designed obscurity of this subject is to cause us to try to "search out the matter", and thus keep our minds concentrated upon the purpose of God.

The points in favour of the Roman application of the time periods are:
(a) That Jesus himself identifies the abomination of desolation as the Roman one.
(b) It was Rome that suppressed the "daily" sacrifices, that destroyed the sanctuary, that devastated the land, and scattered the people. The Moslems continued the desolating, but did not initiate it or do any of these other things.
(c) The Roman system was "set up" by the ambition of the Popes and by the authority of Emperor Phocas.

The Eastern Patriarch Sophronius was just as much an heretical "abomination" as the Moslem invader, if not more so.

The termination of the 1260 and 1290 years with the Fall of the Temporal Power, and the ushering in of the first active steps towards the return of the Jews to their land, proves conclusively that this is the intended application. A further diagram sets out the calculation from the four principal stages of Papal development noted by Guinness.

Characteristic Periods in the Development of God's Purpose
1260 Day-Years
THE LITTLE HORN'S WAR WITH THE SAINTS

A.D. A.D.

Donatist protest against the 312 — 1572 Massacre of St. Bartholomew
apostasy of Constantine; con-
sequent commencement of
persecution of "heretics"

Developing Papal Power		*Declining Papal Power*
1. Decretal letter of Justinian	533 — 1793	French Revolution; Reign of Terror; Louis XVI beheaded; Pope dethroned by Napoleon Bonaparte
2. Accession of Pope Gregory the Great	590 — 1850	Another revolution, 1848; Louis Philippe abdicates; Republic proclaimed; Louis Napoleon proclaimed president
	1849	Pope formally deposed from temporal authority
	1851	Louis Napoleon's coup d'état; Legislative Assembly dissolved
	1852	Prince President declared Emperor = Napoleon III
3. The Edicts and Donations of Phocas	607/ 1867/ 610 — 1870	Decree of Infallibility
4. Accession of Pope Vitalianus	657 — 1917	Palestine freed from Turk; National Home for Jews
His Latinizing decree	663 — 1923	League of Nations Mandate to Britain, July 1922

1290 Day-Years
WAR WITH SAINTS
A.D. 1572 + 30 = 1602   1598   Revocation of Edict of Nantes; Persecution resumed

DECLINE OF TURKISH EMPIRE
Paving way for Jewish National Home

1. 1793 + 30 = 1823   Liberation of Greece; Turkish massacres
2. 1850 + 30 = 1880   Russo-Turkish War
3. 1870 + 30 = 1900   4th Zionist Congress, London
4. 1917 + 30 = 1947-8   State of Israel

CHAPTER 12: APPENDIX III

The Third Vision: The Time Periods and Inspiration

In his books H. Grattan Guinness shows himself very knowledgeable about astronomy, and devotes considerable space to demonstrating the fact that all the time periods introduced into the book of Daniel are lunar-solar cycles. He deduces from this fact a strong argument for the Divine inspiration of the book of Daniel, in that the same hand that created the sun and moon and established their movements, which in turn create the cycles, must have "inspired" the use of those cycles in relation to human history, and the revelation of them in advance to Daniel.

It appears that the existence of these cycles would not have been known to Babylonian astronomy. Here are three quotations from *The Approaching End of the Age*. After demonstrating that both 2300 and 2520 are luni-solar cycles, he continues: "Was it by chance that Daniel lit upon these two periods, so widely dissimilar, and yet which bear to each other *this remarkable astronomic relation*? Impossible! As impossible as that he could either have known that 2300 years (Chapter 8) was a soli-lunar cycle, or that he could have selected by *chance* the exact number of years in that cycle, as the period of the restored temple and subsequent desolation of the sanctuary. Such coincidences are not the work of chance. Such Bible statements must be accepted with reverential awe, as evidences that the Divine mind which planned the universe, inspired also the sacred Book" (p. 443).

"But as the era of miracle receded, the temptation to doubt and unbelief strengthens, and God graciously provided the help of chronological prophecy to sustain to the end the faith and hope of his people. They who in this day despise that aid, or make it void by fanciful, unhistoric futurist interpretations, cast aside an invaluable weapon for the special conflict of these closing days. An age which rejects the argument from miracle, is confronted by that from the fulfilment of prophecy. As the evidence of the *first* becomes more questionable on account of its remote antiquity, that of the *second* becomes more irresistible year by year. Fulfilled prophecy is miracle in the highest sphere—that of the mind. It is the ever growing proof of Divine prescience in the authors of sacred Scripture'' (p. 491).

''The hand of God in history, and the inspiration of prophecy, are clearly attested by this marvellous relation between celestial revolution and chronological periods, which presents also irresistible confirmation of the *year-day* interpretation of the 1260 'days' of prophecy—the assigned duration of the second and more important portion of the 'Times of the Gentiles' '' (p. 669).

EPILOGUE

THOUGH a study of a book purposely sealed up until the time of the end may not have provided us with all the answers, it is to be hoped that it has not been without profit. The unsealing, which has been conveyed to us by the words of the Master in his Mount Olivet Prophecy, and in "The Revelation which God gave unto him", gives us a deeper insight into what God had in mind when He gave His messages to Daniel by the hand of Gabriel.

It was hardly possible to deal adequately with Daniel without making some references to the Mount Olivet Prophecy and the Revelation, but these have been deliberately kept to a minimum, so that concentration could be focused on the earlier book. By this means, one hopes, a desire to study the Mount Olivet Prophecy and Revelation of "Messiah the Prince" will be stimulated in the reader for the future. The reader's attention is directed to some articles in *The Christadelphian* Magazine which may be offered as a "starter". (These will be found in the issues for 1973, p. 173; 1974, p. 539; 1975, January to July; and 1977, February to September.)

God Rules in the Kingdom of Men

Those of us who are older, have seen this principle in action before our eyes. We have seen "powers" and "authorities" removed from their seats and large numbers of the children of Israel return to a land from which they were practically barred for centuries. Unhappily, however, though motivated by idealism, they have returned in "blindness" and in unbelief of Jesus of Nazareth as Messiah. Many of them have gone back ostensibly with the approval of the "Western Powers"; but again unhappily, so restricted in numbers, so much under the pressure of yet another war, and the threat of another "holocaust". The resulting political problems are such that no power on earth can solve them.

The Lord declared through Zechariah: "I will make Jerusalem a burdensome stone for all people: all that burden themselves with it shall be cut in pieces, though all the people of the earth be gathered together against it" (12:3). All Daniel was told, was: "There shall be a time

156

of trouble such as never was.'' Jesus speaks of the kings of the earth and of the whole world being gathered together ''to the battle of that great day of God Almighty . . . And he gathered them together into a place called in the Hebrew tongue Armageddon'' (Revelation 16:14-16).

What great manifestation will it take to tear away the veil of blindness from the eyes of Jewry? What a marvellous privilege has been granted to us, that we are able in these last days to ''understand'' and to be able to say ''We see'', even though only in a limited way? But what tremendous responsibility therefore devolves upon us.

The Bible reveals to us that God *dwells* with His people. His presence was manifested in His Glory in the Holy Place, in the pillar of cloud and fire which guided Israel through their wilderness journey and over-watched their worship at Tabernacle and Temple in the Land. He was compelled to desert the Holy City wherein He had placed His name, because of His people's faithlessness. Do we sense His presence *with us*, invisible though it be? Or do we have a lurking suspicion that much ''revelation'' emanating from the ''Man of the One Spirit'' above the river, manifested in the ''Son of man'' whom God made strong for Himself (Psalm 80:17), still eludes us, leaving our effort inadequate?

Let us strengthen our faith and encourage our hearts with the thought that as God was with Daniel and his three friends in their times of trial, so He will be today with all those who, like Daniel, set their hearts to understand and to humble themselves before their God (Daniel 10:12).

NOTES ON THE CHARTS

Chart No. 1 is an overall diagram of the history involved in the book of Daniel. On the left are B.C. dates of the chief events in reigns of Babylonian kings, and of Cyrus. The reigns according to the Babylonian system of chronology started with an accession year until the first new year, then the first proper year commenced. The Egyptian system numbered the king's first year from the date he ascended the throne. The Biblical record conforms to either system according to whether the influence of Egypt or of Babylon was paramount over the Jews at the time. Hence the second column quotes the year under both systems. The column headed "The Fall of Jerusalem" indicates the death of King Josiah, the reign of Jehoiakim for 11 years, the captivity of Jehoiachin, the reign of Zedekiah for 11 years, the second captivity; and indicates how the period of 70 years prophesied by Jeremiah worked out. The dreams and visions of Nebuchadnezzar and Daniel are pointed out at the dates when they were given, and brief notes of their purport are given at the right-hand side.

Chart No. 2 gives the earlier part of the period covered in Chart 1 in greater detail, to illustrate the chapter and appendix dealing with the historical background to the book of Daniel. The accession dated years start from a different month from the Babylonian years, hence an overlap; so they are indicated *between* the years of the reigns of Nabopolassar and Nebuchadnezzar. The estimate of the age of Daniel is based on the assumption (which may not be correct) that he commenced his mission at the age of 30, as Ezekiel appears to have done (Ezekiel 1:1); and there are other precedents, notably the Lord Jesus. The second column is based on the assumption that he was 30 when he interpreted the dream of Nebuchadnezzar. This makes out a reasonable age for his upbringing in a Jewish environment, but very old when he had the vision of chapters 10-12. There is a Jewish tradition that the "second year of Nebuchadnezzar", when he had the dream of the golden-headed image, was his second year *as king over Jerusalem*. If Daniel was aged 30 *then*, the difficulty about the shortness of time for his three years Chaldean training before appearing before

Nebuchadnezzar is overcome, but he would have been very young to be used as a hostage, and how did he acquire his faith in the God of Israel? The figures for this interprepation are as shown in column 1.

Chart No. 3 illustrates chapter 9, the prophecy of the 70 weeks, which equals 490 years, calculated from the four appropriate decrees (and also chapter 12, which contains the time periods of 3½ times, 1290 and 1335 days).

Chart No. 4 summarises the application of Daniel's dream and visions.

Chart No. 5 is a comparison between the subject matter of the first six chapters, which concern the dreams and activities of the Babylonian and Persian kings, of whom Daniel was *a subject*; and the second six chapters in which Daniel relates *his* dream and visions granted him by God. There is a fairly clear correspondence which shows through better by tabulation than by verbal description.

CHART NO. 1: HISTORICAL BACKGROUND

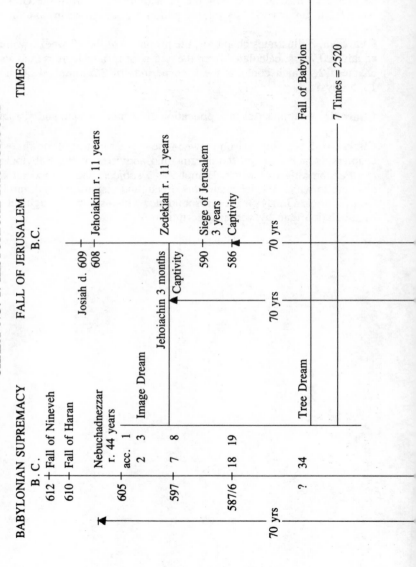

BABYLONIAN SUPREMACY	FALL OF JERUSALEM	TIMES
B.C.	B.C.	
612 — Fall of Nineveh		
610 — Fall of Haran	Josiah d. 609	
	608 — Jehoiakim r. 11 years	
Nebuchadnezzar r. 44 years		
605 — acc. 1		
2 3 — Image Dream		
	Jehoiachin 3 months	
597 — 7 8	Captivity	Zedekiah r. 11 years
	590 — Siege of Jerusalem 3 years	
587/6 — 18 19	586 — Captivity	
	70 yrs	70 yrs
? — 34	Tree Dream	Fall of Babylon
70 yrs		7 Times = 2520

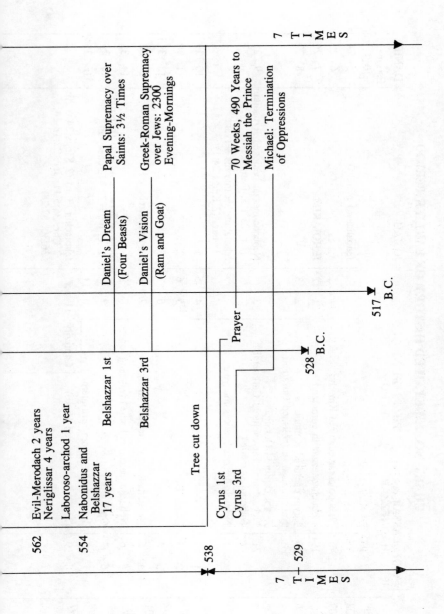

562 | Evil-Merodach 2 years
Neriglissar 4 years
Laboroso-archod 1 year

554 | Nabonidus and
Belshazzar
17 years

Belshazzar 1st — Daniel's Dream — Papal Supremacy over
(Four Beasts) Saints: 3½ Times

Belshazzar 3rd — Daniel's Vision — Greek-Roman Supremacy
(Ram and Goat) over Jews: 2300
Evening-Mornings

Tree cut down

Cyrus 1st — Prayer — 70 Weeks, 490 Years to
Cyrus 3rd Messiah the Prince

Michael: Termination
of Oppressions

538 | 528 B.C. | 517 B.C.

529

7 TIMES

7 TIMES

CHART NO. 2: DETAILED HISTORY OF EARLIER PERIOD

B.C.	NABOPOLASSAR & NEBUCHADNEZZAR	v. PHARAOH NECHO	JOSIAH	DANIEL	Estimated Age
609			died		
608		acc. 1	Jehoahaz (3 months)	5	24
607	19th Nabopolassar captured Kimuhu / 19 Nebuchadnezzar in command	1	2 JEHOIAKIM	6	25
606	20 Egypt captured Kimuhu / Nabopolassar established Quramati	2	3	7	26
605	21 Egypt captured Quramati / Nebuchadnezzar captured Carchemish / Nabopolassar died	3	4	8	27
604	acc. 1 Nebuchadnezzar's accession year	4	5 Nebuchadnezzar besieged Jerusalem (Jer. 25:1,3; Dan. 1:1) — Jehoiakim became his servant 3 years (2 Kings 24:1)	9	28
603	1	5	6	10	29
602	2 Image Dream	6	7	11	30
601	3	7	8	12	31
600	4 Nebuchadnezzar defeated in Egypt	8	9 Jehoiakim rebelled	13	32
599	5 Nebuchadnezzar at home mustering forces	9	10	14	33
598	6 Operations in Syria	10	11 Siege of Jerusalem; Jehoiakim died Dec. 6/7 = 22 Marcheswan	15	34
597	7 3023 captives from Jerusalem / 8 (2nd Adar = March 15/16) / 9	11 acc.	acc. Captivity — Jehoiachin (3 m) (2 Kings 24:6-20; 2 Chr. 36:5-11; Jer. 22:18-24; 36:30; 52:28)	16	35

ZEDEKIAH

B.C.						ZEDEKIAH	
596	9	10	1	1	(7 years)	18	37
			·	·		·	·
588	17	18	9	9	832 captives	27	46
587	18	19	10	10	Siege and Fall of Jerusalem (Jer. 52:4-12,28; 2 Kings 25:1-2; 2 Chron. 26:13; Jer. 37)	28	47
586	19	20	11	11		29	48
585	20	21	12		1 Captivity	30	49
584	21	22	13		2nd of Nebuchadnezzar over Jerusalem	31	50
583	22	23	14		3	32	51
582	23	24	15		745 captives / 4		
			·		(45 years)	·	·
536	3rd		CYRUS			78	97

(7 years)

(45 years)

70 YEAR PERIODS

	B.C.	B.C.	
Fall of Assyria at Haran	610-9	539	Fall of Babylon
Captivity of Jehoiachin	597	528	1st Cambyses (death of Cyrus)
Siege of Jerusalem	590	520	Restart building Temple
Captivity of Zedekiah	587-6	516	Temple finished
Finished Temple	516	444	20th Artaxerxes (Nehemiah)

CHART NO. 3: RESTORATION OF JERUSALEM UNTO MESSIAH

DARIUS

1st   Daniel's Prayer answered by Prophecy of 70 Weeks = 490 years

Decrees

			B.C.	
1.	1st Cyrus	Sheshbazzar	538	Altar built
	3rd Cyrus	Zerubbabel	536	Temple foundation laid
2.	2nd Darius Hystaspes		520	Temple building resumed
	6th Darius Hystaspes		516	Temple finished
3.	7th Artaxerxes	Ezra	457+490 solar = A.D. 34 ? Jesus born 6-4 B.C.; crucified A.D. 28-30	
4.	20th Artaxerxes	Nehemiah	444+486½ lunar to midst of week = 472 solar; crucified A.D. 29	

CHART NO. 4: DANIEL'S DREAM AND VISIONS

BELSHAZZAR
1st Year   Four Beasts
552/1 B.C.   Ch. 7

1. *Papal Supremacy over Saints*
   3½ Times: A.D. 606/10 + 1260
         = A.D. 1866/1870

BELSHAZZAR
3rd Year   Ram &
550/49 B.C.   He-Goat
             Ch. 8

2. *Greek-Roman Supremacy over Jews*
   2300 Evening-Mornings

	B.C.	A.D.
Persia overthrown	330 —	1971
Alexander died	323 —	1978
Four Horns begin	301 —	2000
(Battle of Ipsus)		

DARIUS
1st Year   Prayer
538 B.C.   70 Weeks
            Ch. 9

3. *To Messiah the Prince*
   490 years = 7th Artaxerxes
       457 B.C. — A.D. 33 incl.;
   midst of last week 27-33 B.C.
   (therefore crucified A.D. 29½, aged
       33½; born 4 B.C.)

CYRUS
3rd Year   Michael
536 B.C.   Ch. 10-12

4. *Resurrection: Termination of*
       Oppressions
   (a) 3½ Times: same as Ch. 7
       A.D. 606/10 + 1260 = 1866/1870
       Fall of Temporal Power of Papacy

   (b) 1290: A.D. 606/10 + 1290 = 1897/1900
       Zionist Congresses

   (c) 1335 Anno Hegira (lunar) = A.D. 1917
       Turks ousted from Palestine; Hegira
       Calendar ended; another application
       still to come
       1967: Jerusalem re-united
       1978: Israel, peace with Egypt;
                invasion of Lebanon

CHART NO. 5: COMPARATIVE VISIONS

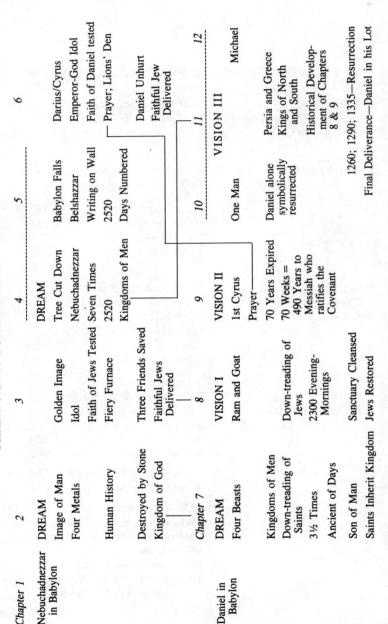

Chapter 1	2	3	4	5	6
Nebuchadnezzar in Babylon	DREAM		DREAM		
	Image of Man	Golden Image	Tree Cut Down	Babylon Falls	Darius/Cyrus
	Four Metals	Idol	Nebuchadnezzar	Belshazzar	Emperor-God Idol
		Faith of Jews Tested	Seven Times	Writing on Wall	Faith of Daniel tested
	Human History	Fiery Furnace	2520	2520	Prayer; Lions' Den
			Kingdoms of Men	Days Numbered	
	Destroyed by Stone	Three Friends Saved			Daniel Unhurt
	Kingdom of God	Faithful Jews Delivered			Faithful Jew Delivered

Chapter 7	8	9	10	11	12
Daniel in Babylon					
DREAM	VISION I	VISION II	VISION III		Michael
Four Beasts	Ram and Goat	1st Cyrus	One Man		
		Prayer		Persia and Greece	
Kingdoms of Men		70 Years Expired	Daniel alone symbolically resurrected	Kings of North and South	
Down-treading of Saints	Down-treading of Jews	70 Weeks = 490 Years to Messiah who ratifies the Covenant			
3½ Times	2300 Evening-Mornings			Historical Development of Chapters 8 & 9	
Ancient of Days					
Son of Man	Sanctuary Cleansed			1260; 1290; 1335—Resurrection	
Saints Inherit Kingdom	Jews Restored			Final Deliverance—Daniel in his Lot	